OUT ON A CLIFF

EARLY PRAISES FOR OUT ON A CLIFF

Gary Rubie was a cops cop. His portrayal of the horrors of police work is masterful. From the stench of death to the loneliness and desensitizing effect of the job. He bares all about a job he once loved, but came to loathe. His words accurately describe an occupation designed not only to create psychological victims, but occupational casualties. He takes the lid off the Pandora's box of policing and allows us to peek inside. He's a survivor. Gary should probably be dead—but for God—and the purpose that God has for his life.

~ Chief of Police Daniel C. Parkinson, M.O.M., Cornwall Community Police Service, Cornwall, Ontario, Canada ~

Painful, captivating, don't put it down until you finish. This is a book of pain, courage and hope. It is a story that takes the reader along a painful journey of the darkest psyche of abuse and addiction where the unconscious mind seduces and holds hostage the darkest shadows of the soul. And in that darkness, Gary finds the strength to sit in his pain, embrace his shadows, trust his heart and free his soul. Through his process, Gary cultivates brilliant consciousness and transformation, illuminating his path, his heart, and his story with inspiration.

~ Diana Lockett, M.Sc., R-EYT, Founder and Director of Inspire Yoga Studios Canada. ~

An intensely evocative, heart-wrenching, profoundly courageous act of self-revealing. This book pulls no punches, inviting us to sit in the liberating discomfort of another's truths. Rubie takes off the mask of shame that imprisons incest survivors and addicts, and invites us all to brave his revealing. I felt free to be entirely real about my own life after reading this book. Such a brave piece of art!

~ Jeff Brown
Author of Soulshaping: A Journey of Self-Creation~

Out on a Cliff is not an easy read. For me, however, the images of pain, rage and despair had special meaning. I worked with Gary during his 18 month battle to have his PTSD recognized as work-related. I was the one who prevailed upon him to write an account of his trauma that almost killed him; but ultimately it was that account that established the link between emotional decline, his addiction and his work.

Gary's work in Out on a Cliff represents for me tangible evidence of both the frailty and indomitable spirit of this gentle man. His poetry evokes an almost child-like attempt to identify his demons and confront them. The artwork by his father demonstrates an intuitive understanding of his son's pain, as well as a father's realization that time and events have not dulled the need to help a son through a time of great angst.

As you read this book, you will continually feel a need to reconcile Rubie's poetry and the vulnerability it depicts on the one hand, and his years of being "out there" serving and protecting you and I, on the other. The price he has paid is enormous; and yet the gift he presents to those many others in police work who may themselves feel the gnawing pangs of PTSD is priceless.

~ Mr. Andy Emmink, Paralegal, A. Emmink Professional Corporation,
Ajax, Ontario, Canada

The only way people can find and walk the path to unconditional love and self healing is through complete transparency. First with themselves, then with others. Gary Rubie has courageously walked himself through this process through his poetry and now offers everyone who reads and reflects on this collection the opportunity to do the same.

~ Dr. Peter J. Amlinger, DC
Amlinger Family Chiropractic Centre
2006 Independent Canadian Chiropractor of the Year
President Purposeful Living Inc.
Mississauga, Ontario, Canada

OUT ON A CLIFF

A city cop tells his story of abuse, addiction,
P.T.S.D., and recovery in poetry and illustration

WRITTEN BY GARY RUBIE

Illustrations by Henk Rubie

Foreword by Dr. Harry Vedelago, MSc., MD, CCFP, FCFP, ASAM, ABAM

Copyright © 2012 by Gary Rubie and Henk Rubie.

Library of Congress Control Number:		2012904340
ISBN:	Hardcover	978-1-4691-8115-8
	Softcover	978-1-4691-8114-1
	Ebook	978-1-4691-8116-5

All rights reserved. No part of this book may be reproduced or transmitted in any form or by any means, electronic or mechanical, including photocopying, recording, or by any information storage and retrieval system, without permission in writing from the copyright owner.

This book was printed in the United States of America.

To order additional copies of this book, contact:
Xlibris Corporation
1-888-795-4274
www.Xlibris.com
Orders@Xlibris.com
111404

DEDICATION

I would like to thank my parents for being the best parents they could be in raising my sister, my brother, and me. You would be hard-pressed to find two more caring and loving people on the planet. A testament to their love for each other is recently celebrating their fifty-third wedding anniversary. They always encouraged me to pursue what I believed was right, and I followed that direction to a fault. Thank you, Dad and Mom! Please know that most of the hardships in my life were job related or self-inflicted; *they had nothing to do with either of you.* An extra special thank you to my father, who (since retiring twenty-one years ago) further honed his skills as an artist, oil painter, and boatbuilder and completed all the illustrations for this book, including the cover. My little brother, Frank, and older sister, Diana, you have always been there to prop me back up and encourage me to carry on when I would fall yet again into the devil's hands. Thank you.

I must also recognize my friend CJ, the angel from the A&P, the lady that was placed into my life to walk through some of the darkest times so I wouldn't have to *go it alone*. You didn't understand policing, PTSD, or dual addictions, nor did you understand the many other disorders, but you walked with me and made my journey less painful. For now, I must walk alone. Thank you.

This book is further dedicated to all the men and women out there who endured abuse in their lives, whether it was emotional, mental, physical, or sexual. I further dedicate this book to the men and women in blue, who serve and protect our asses every day and who may have suffered from an abusive process and P.T.S.D.

To my friend Langer, you guided me to the doors and waited with loyalty until I entered. And to my sponsor Jack, you were the calm, cool breeze surrounding me while I stood in the eye of the tornado. I thank you both, my two amigos.

To my niece Ashley for allowing me to use the poem you wrote for me on my fortieth birthday to close this book. As an eighteen-year-old high school student, you captured my life's journey, sharing wisdom far, far beyond your years. Somehow you encapsulated my life ten years ago, and I hadn't even reached my darkest moment yet. You have provided me with closure for this project. I continue to live and face challenges, but when I read your poem, I'm taken out of myself. Thank you, and I love you.

To "J," thank you for two beautiful daughters.

To Ms. Wendy Woo for *crawling inside my head unarmed*, a place I couldn't enter alone.

To Dr. Harry Vedelago for sharing your wisdom and for believing in me; you continue to treat and support me. You were the perfect choice to write the foreword to this book. In friendship and undying loyalty, thank you, Doc.

To my children, Kirstyn and Nicole (Nikki), a million "I'm sorrys" could never erase the shameful memories you had to endure at one time or another and have to carry for the rest of your lives. I love you both with every fiber of my being. If I could take it all back, I would. *Yesterday, Today, and Tomorrow.*

> *To every victim of P.T.S.D., alcoholic and addict that suffered, recovered, and still suffers,* I hope for serenity, courage, wisdom.

CONTENTS

DEDICATION vii
FOREWORD xiii
INTRODUCTION xvii

GROWING UP / ABUSE 1

SEIZURE 2
ABUSED 4
NEVER 6
I FELL DOWN THE CHURCH STAIRS 8
INNOCENCE TAKEN 10
THE ANNEX 12
SCARS 14
HELP 16

RELATIONSHIPS 19

MA 20
DIANA 22
FRANK 26
THE TOWERS TAKE TWO 30
BIG YELLOW 32
FOREVER IN MY HEART 34
THE END 38
THE GRAND CANYON 40
A MEMORY 42
THE TIES THAT BIND 44
BABY BLUE 46
THE NIKKI POEM 48
GYPSY ON THE DRIP 50
GOOD-BYE, MY FRIEND 54
R 2 CC 56
SKITTER-BUG 58
THE PORCH 60
ME AND MY GIRL 62
UNDERSTANDING 64
WHEN YOU . . . I FEEL . . . I NEED 66

ANGEL FROM THE A&P—CHAPTER 1 68
ANGEL FROM THE A&P—CHAPTER 2 69
ANGEL FROM THE A&P—CHAPTER 3 70
ANGEL FROM THE A&P—CHAPTER 4 71
YOU TAUGHT ME 72
ANOTHER RELATIONSHIP 74
THE SUNSET 76
ANGEL FROM THE A&P—FINAL CHAPTER 78

POLICING 81

MY FIRST YEAR 82
TOOLS OF MY TRADE 84
SCOTTY 86
NIGHTS 88
SUBPOENA DELIVERY 90
HUNGOVER 92
DEAD ON THE FLOOR OF A BUS 94
OLD MAN 96
THE TAXI 98
HOW CLOSE YOU CAME 100
THE PLAY 102
THE CALLBACK 104
BROKEN 106
YOUR REIGN OF TERROR 108
THE STRUCTURE 110
ALL TAKE AND NO GIVE 112
CHILD PORN 114
NUMB 116
THE JUNTAS 118
RATS WITH HATS 120
NO REGRETS 122
MY CAREER (1133) 124
UNTOUCHABLE EGO 126
MY PAIN 128
PTSD 130

ADDICTIONS 133

ROUND AND ROUND 134
THE MORNING DRINK THE EVENING HANGOVER 136
BRIGS AND BENNY 138
CLOSET 140

x

BARSTOOL	142
THE DARKNESS	144
STAIRCASE TO HELL	146
RELAPSE	148
REFLECTION	150
INSANITY DEFINED	152
WATER UNDER THE BRIDGE	154
REAPER TAKER	156
THE DEVIL	158
MARY JANE	160
BETWEEN THE LINES	162
COMIN' DOWN	164
IN MY HEAD	166
MY STRUGGLES	168
SELFISH	170
SWALLOWED UP	172
FGI	174
ONE STEP, TWO	176
WHAT I SEE (PEDDLERS ON THE BEACH)	178
LINES ON MY FACE	180
40-40	182
ON THE EDGE OF THE CLIFF	184
LOSE IT	186
LAST WALTZ	188
SEGREGATION	190
MY FRIEND (LANGER)	192

TREATMENT / RECOVERY **195**

TREATMENT	196
TAKING THAT STEP	198
THE HOLE	200
STORM	202
ALPHA ROOM	204
CLOSED N.A.	206
THE CIRCLE	208
STEP UP TO THE PLATE	210
BALANCE AND STRUCTURE	212
P.V. MEXICO	214
STRANGLEHOLD	216
ANXIETY	218
EYES	220
2009	222

MEDS	224
THE STAIRCASE	226
INSOMNIA	228
DRY DRUNK	230
YESTERDAY	232
TRAPPED IN A TUNNEL	234
DEAR GOD	236
EAGLE SPIRIT	238
CLOUD	240
THE GAMBLE	242
THE YARD	244
PENTHOUSE 11	246
GROUNDED	248
PORT OF MIAMI	250
MY PAST	252
WHAT'S MY FUTURE?	254
THE W.S.I.B. INTERVIEW	256
HOW TO RECOVER	258
A CANVAS	260
A CLEAR HEAD	262
MAYBE NEXT TIME I'LL GET IT RIGHT	264
ROUND THREE TREATMENT	266
GOOD-BYE, ADDICTION	268
THE TRANSFORMATION	270
THE MASTERPIECE	272
CIRCA 1940	274
THE VISIT	276
SURRENDER	278
BREAKING THROUGH THE OTHER SIDE	280
THE ILLUSTRATOR	282
YOUR CIRCLE	284
CONCLUSION	285
GOODBYE	287
INDEX	289
AUTHOR'S PROFILE	295

FOREWORD

I have come across many patients over the past ten years as a physician specializing in the treatment of addictions. The majority of those I treat leave me with a faded memory that over time becomes an interesting anecdote. There are very few patients that I remember vividly. The nature of my work requires a certain detachment if one is to retain one's sense of objectivity and sanity. There are, however, those exceptions that do stay with me. Gary Rubie is one.

I first heard of Gary in the late summer of 2010. A colleague of mine, Ms. Wendi Woo, asked me if I would do her a favor and accept a patient scheduled to be admitted to our hospital. She had treated him previously for Post-Traumatic Stress Disorder and it was her opinion that my therapeutic style would fit this patient's needs perfectly. I knew that I had no choice. My acceptance was a foregone conclusion. I owed this colleague much for her clinical help in the past and now she was calling in her favors.

I reviewed the information on this Mr. Rubie and my heart sank. My colleague is not prone to exaggeration and the diagnosis of severe PTSD and addiction was not given lightly. She could see the dread in my face and told me to give him a chance.

Gary walked into my office on October 19, 2010. There are three things from this first meeting that I noticed immediately; his height, his inability to stop shaking and his eyes. Of all these, it is his eyes that have remained in my memory ever since; for they had the look of naked misery.

In my time I have heard many tragic stories, have had patients shed countless tears but misery, in its purest form, is rare. Misery is a desert where the capacity to shed tears has vanished and where screams are muffled by the suffocating despair of hopelessness. On this day in October misery was staring back at me.

I admit that at first I truly believed that Gary was beyond my help. His PTSD complicated by his addiction was so severe that death by his own hand would likely be his lot.

"I'll do anything you ask Doc".

It was these words that Gary uttered in the middle of our first meeting that gave me hope that together we might just pull it off; that he just might make it.

It has been 18 months since my first meeting with Gary. I continue to follow him as a patient of mine. His gratitude for the gift of recovery is expressed at the end of each of our appointments. It is Gary, however, who has given me more than I could ever give him. He has given me the gift in joining him through his journey of recovery. To witness a miracle of recovery as it unfolds.

Within the pages of this book the life of Gary Rubie is presented to you. It is an invitation. An invitation to join the journey of recovery as it unfolds. Enjoy the ride. I have.

H.R. Vedelago MD

Doctor Harry Vedelago, MSc., MD, CCFP, FCFP, ASAM, ABAM is licensed to practice medicine in the Province of Ontario. He remains in good standing with The College of Physicians and Surgeons and is a Fellow of The College of Family Physicians of Canada. He is certified by the American Society of Addiction Medicine and is a Diplomat of the American Board of Addiction Medicine. Dr. Vedelago is the senior staff physician at the Homewood Health Centre, Addiction Division in Guelph, Ontario, Canada. His is also an Associate Professor (adjunct) with the Department of Family Medicine at McMaster University, Hamilton, Ontario, Canada.

Dr. Harry Vedelago, MSc., MD, CCFP, FCFP, ASAM, ABAM
Homewood Health Centre
Senior Staff Physician
Addiction Division
Guelph, Ontario, Canada

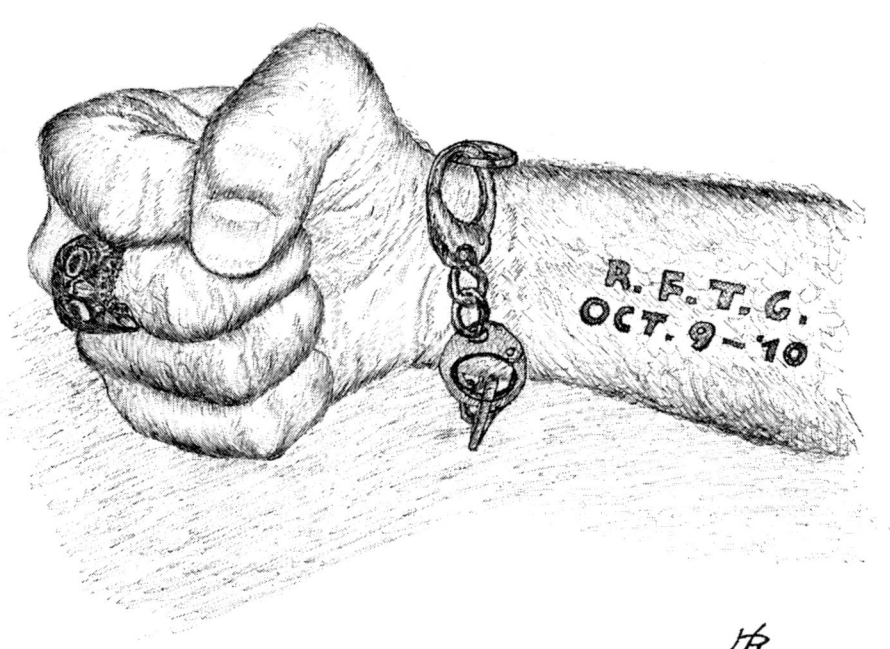

RISEN FROM THE GRAVE

INTRODUCTION

The following poems will take you on an intense journey to the center of the author's mind, my mind, and you will peek into the darkest hole in my soul. All the poems (stories) are based on real-life experiences, all lived and experienced by me.

The poems range from growing up, being abused, into a twenty-seven-year career in policing, (which caused P.T.S.D. and led me to Suicide attempts), to going through my addictions and recovery. All the poems are complemented by illustrations, completed in collaboration with my father, Henk Rubie. These poems and illustrations are A REFELCTION OF WHO I AM. They are my life; they are where I've been, what I've done, where I've come from, and where I don't ever want to go back to. This is my memoir.

Because of the many negative childhood and policing experiences, the very thing that almost killed me (my addictions) actually saved my life. My addictions took me out of my own head and let me live in a different world. One that slowly and methodically dulled the pain of my existence but was also slowly killing me.

I knew that if I wasn't able to have one more drink, one more hit, I would just die. I also knew that if I continued using, it was going to kill me. Only the addict understands this degree of despair and darkness. I had to learn a different way of living, one that was foreign to me. Two treatment centers, five programs, eleven years of soul-searching, and making the final decision. Do I want to live under certain terms and conditions, or do I want to die? I chose death. When I failed at that, it became apparent that my great Eagle Spirit had different plans for me.

If one poem touches one person and stops that one person from ending their life, or gives one person hope, or keeps one person sober for one day, then all the hard work, honesty, and hours of painful soul-searching that went into creating this book was worth it. *Godspeed.*

GARY RUBIE AND HENK RUBIE

May the road rise to meet you, May the wind be always at your back, May the sun shine warm upon your face, The rains fall soft upon your fields and, Until by chance we ever meet, May God hold you in the palm of His hand. (An Irish blessing)

  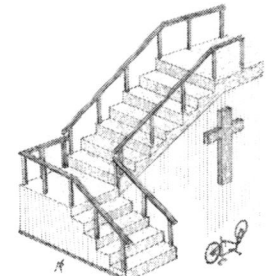

GROWING UP / ABUSE

  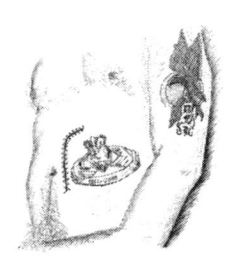

SEIZURE

Swallowed my tongue, started to shake
Foam from the mouth, couldn't get me awake

Fingers in the mouth, cleared the throat
Mom placed the call to the man in the white coat

One white-haired man saved my life
The other white-haired man carried a knife

The foam didn't stop, wrapped in a blanket to keep me warm
But the man with the knife took me back to where I was born

Everyone there had a white coat on
Could a two-year-old boy be this far gone?

So they locked me up in a silver cage
It was in this cage that I learned to rage

Please let me come home; I promise to behave
If you leave me here, I may end up in a grave

Sad . . . scared . . . isolated . . . alone . . .
Mommy, I love you; can I please come home?

So they watched my tiny head to see if it would flicker
It was likely then that I became prone to liquor

Only after two weeks, I finally went home
But for forty-four years, I remained all alone

All alone to fight the battles and pain
That started that day with a twitch in my brain

Out On A Cliff

ABUSED

I know your pain; it sears like a knife
You never expected this to happen in your life

You were young like me, full of love and trust
Like an insect in a web, became victim to his lust

How could you escape? You were just so small
You couldn't stop him, he was big and tall

An adult stealing away the most precious thing of all
A young child's innocence, and like a beast, he'd maul

I was only five years old, and it changed my life forever
Attempts on my life, dysfunctional relationships, stormy weather

As I got older, booze and dope killed the pain
But I paid the price of addiction and damaged my brain

So many years, I wished I was dead
But instead I altered the chemicals in my head

Was suicide the answer, would that stop the rage?
Make it quick and painless, or rot my life in a cage

So much blaming; hey, it wasn't my fault
It was time to lock this nightmare into a vault

But that didn't work either; I had to let go
Let go of the beast, let go of the woe

For forty-one years, it tore me apart
I've come to forgive from deep in my heart

I know your pain; it sears like a knife
You never expected this to happen in your life

Out On A Cliff

NEVER

What were you thinking when you took it away?
Did life hand you your own set of rules?
A child's innocence led so far astray
Played us all like we were such damn fools

Why did they allow this to happen?
Was gonna hate them both for life
Two people who believed in the Chaplain
Forty-four long years of strife

I fell down and awoke on the floor
I'd show them the result of my pain
I knocked hard on heaven's front door
I'd have to come back and knock once again

Forty-four years was my sentence
Driving down life's highway at 210
Always asking for God's repentance
I would ask again and again and again

I forgave the two who truly loved me
How could they know what had gone on?
A light shone from far above me
This trip had gone on for too long

When my mind finally tired of asking
I surrendered to all the pain
Who knew it could be this lasting?
Never driving down that highway again
Never driving down that highway again
Never

Out On A Cliff

I FELL DOWN THE CHURCH STAIRS

I fell down the church stairs but didn't feel the pain
Were the sensors completely shut deep down in my brain?

Got up and walked, put my bike against the wall
It was a wicked tumble, couldn't believe the fall

Came into the church, just joined the Boy Scouts
Walked down the basement, followed the sounds of the shouts

I think I was dazed or just afraid to tell
Daddy might smack me, going straight to hell

So just another incident I buried away
It would help me to live for just another day

You see, I was haunted from a very young age
So I avoided all chances of being caught in the rage

Just another event in my formative years
That I would learn to bury with a few dozen beers

The Boy Scouts gave me a safe place to be
Fishing and camping and climbing a tree

When I look back upon the time that I had
I am really lucky that I did have a dad

'Cause most of those kids didn't have a dad at home
They lived with their moms and sisters alone

They didn't have dads who would teach them to camp
They slept with the lights on, protected by a lamp

So watch out for the stairs in the old church halls
Or you'll end up like me and take a big fall

Out On A Cliff

Gary Rubie and Henk Rubie

INNOCENCE TAKEN

Remember when we lay out on the grass
Jumped lines on the sidewalk; don't break Mother's back

We'd lie and stare up as the clouds drifted by
There were lions and tigers—entire zoos in the sky

Man, those were the days when jelly beans and hockey cards
Meant more to me than a truckload of gold bars

But things quickly changed, and the innocence was gone
It happened so quick, it didn't take long

When my innocence was taken, it was like a noose around my neck
I carried it for over forty years; it turned me into a wreck

It took a lot of help from others to get me well
If I hadn't taken what they offered me, I'd have gone straight to hell

That kind of pain doesn't disappear; it lurks inside your head
You gotta make it go away, or you'll end up being dead

Today I stare up at the stars and see the Milky Way
I know they're real and they taste like chocolate; I want it to stay that way

If someone stole your innocence and you want it to return
It won't come back all by itself; it's something you have to earn

Work hard at making yourself feel good
Lie on the grass in your neighborhood

And while you're there, look up to the sky
Seeing the entire zoo will make you cry

The tears you shed will be those of joy
And just for the moment, you'll be that little boy

You will have recovered because you endured
And the pain you once felt will be finally cured

Out On A Cliff

Gary Rubie and Henk Rubie

THE ANNEX

Suckered to the head, knocked to the ground
Boots to the face, lucky I was found

Pulled myself up, couldn't see through the blood
Nose was shattered, face felt like mud

A man half my size went into a fury
The attack was quick, then he left in a hurry

Trauma to the brain affects how you think
Distorts all your thoughts, makes you want to drink

I was asked how it happened, didn't have an answer
Fear went through me like a stage 4 cancer

Go find the girl; she'll tell you how it went
She'll tell you how the last moments were spent

So the cops took statements and some pictures of my head
They took notes of my injuries, said I was lucky I wasn't dead

Work boots to the face really left a deep scar
But once the cut's healed, I still felt bizarre

The trial was long; they put my name on the line
Crown Attorney told me not to worry, said all would be fine

The little man was convicted, got sixty in the clink
Took the jury a while; the case made them think

A civil trial followed, but by then I didn't care
My new career had started, got a gun and short hair

For many years after, the anxiety remained
When I drank to forget thought of a .38 to the brain

Those days are behind, but the memories still there
Of that Oktoberfest night when life wasn't fair

Out On A Cliff

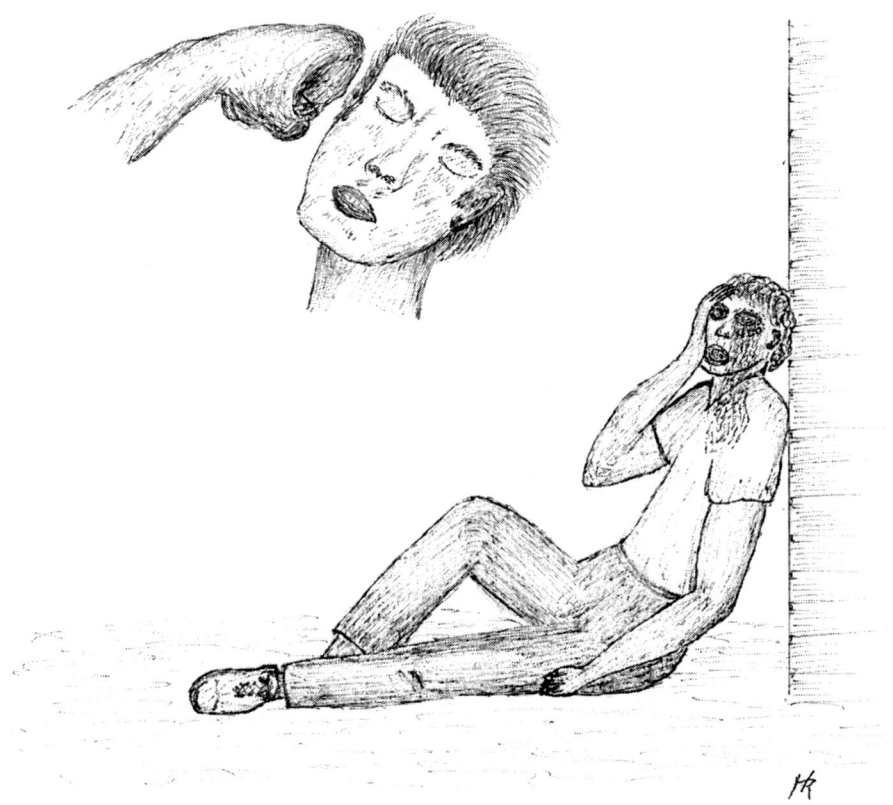

SCARS

Scars on my knees, scars on my face
Shoulder has a zipper, I am not a disgrace

That's just the way my body was built
Take all the hurt, carry the guilt

Show them to anyone who cares to look
Like most of intrigue, it's the cover of a book

Covered the hurt with tattoos and ink
No one can judge me, no need to think

You never walked a mile in my shoes
If you even tried, you'd probably lose

Scars remind us of where we've been
The paint on bodies depicting each scene

But my scars are fresh, yet they don't bleed
I've come to accept that I'm just a different breed

I won't judge you, so don't judge me
When scars and ink are all that you see

**Out of suffering have emerged the strongest souls;
the most massive character are seared with scars. (E. H. Chapin)**

Out On A Cliff

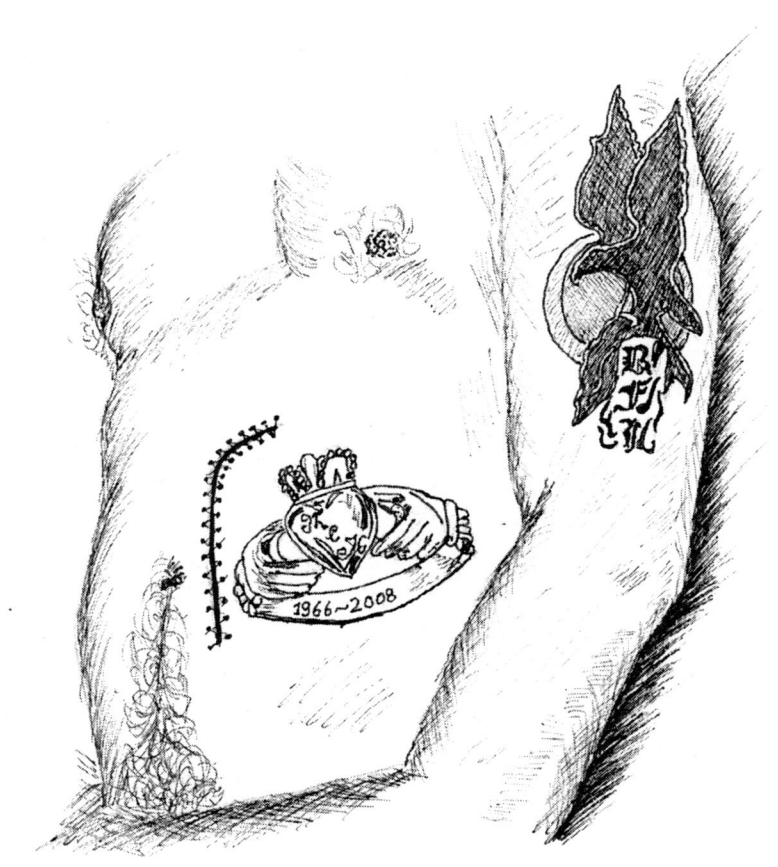

HELP

I asked for help; you arrived at the door
I cried and I wept and I fell to the floor

You picked me up, held my head up high
You said it wasn't my time to die

Followed my friend Michael through another door
The prophet who was there dropped me to the floor

I spoke to Jesus two times that day
He told me I had a great deal to say

A lot to share with my fellow preachers
He said I would become a brand-new teacher

I was not to listen to the wall of hate
My road was paved to the pearly gate

Just follow his word, do not fear
And just stay away from the demonic first beer

Stray not from the path, and all will be well
And keep your soul from the gates of hell

Out On A Cliff

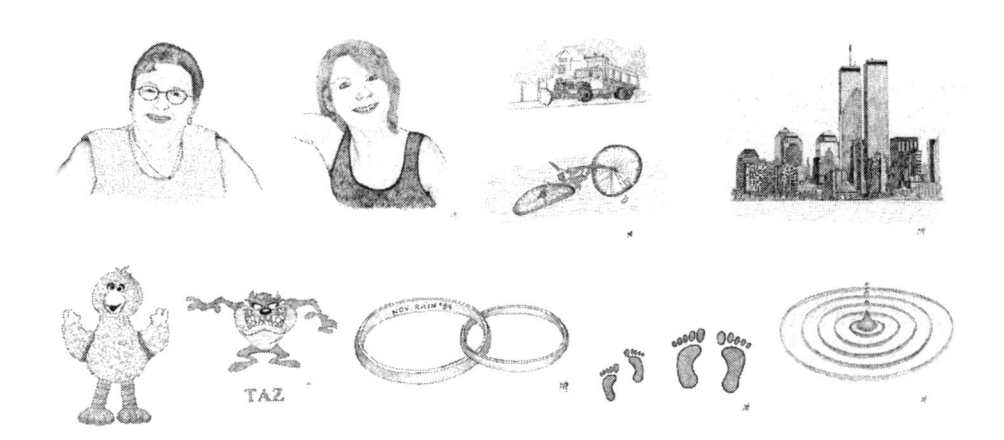

RELATIONSHIPS

Gary Rubie and Henk Rubie

MA

Ma, you are wicked strong; you held us together
When lightning would strike, you protected us from the weather

Three hot meals a day, and always so good
You cooked on gas or over wood

When I was a little boy, you chased the bullies away
You made the neighborhood safe for me to play

You were my biggest fan when we went to the rink
You told me "Don't fight, play fair, and think"

When I first broke my nose, you held the towel on my face
Dad drove us fast to the hospital for stitches and tape

I remember later that day, while I rested you sang
"Funny face, I love you" along with the vinyl and turntable twang

High school came and went, and off to college I ran
Gave you and a few gray hairs, I thought it looked good with your tan

Gave you a scare at Oktoberfest one year
Was a sign of things to come from Mr. Barleycorn the beer

Then the day came when, with my suitcase, I drove away
You put on a brave face, and through tears you waved

Starting my career as a cop, gonna fix the whole planet
You prayed each day for my safe return to stay strong as granite

Twenty-six years passed, and many stories got buried
You supported me through it all, fickle friends, I got married

But now I'm here because I'm not all there
Your little boy's come home for his Ma's love and care

I love you, Ma!

Out On A Cliff

DIANA

Got an older sister; her name is Diana
She's always been my number one fan

She's got a heart that's big as a mountain
Has energy so high, like she drank from the youth fountain

When we were kids, we fought like crazy
After we went to Holland, she became a daisy

We both grew up on that trip with Mom
It's safe to say we had a lot of fun

The next two years we grew very close
Walked to school together; she was my rose

I protected her and our Rubie name
Fought with an older kid for a reason the same

She met a man, and I took her to the station
Was taking the train out west; it brought her elation

I was very sad and felt all alone
My world had changed, entered a different zone

Another year went by; I had a chance to see her
Drove west with another guy; the trip was a blur

God himself couldn't have planned a better arrival
She didn't know I was coming to visit her survival

Out On A Cliff

There she stood, right there before my eyes
It was 5:00 p.m. in Calgary; I tell you no lies

"Hey, good looking!" I yelled from afar
She stumbled and screamed and ran from her car

She jumped into my arms; I had a lump in my throat
It was like a scene from a movie that neither of us wrote

"Get a room!" yelled a passerby, and others clapped
It was such a special moment; I was all alone, completely wrapped

That was a great visit, then I had to go home
And then that empty darkness made me feel all alone

She moved back home not long after that
It's safe to say that on her couch I often sat

Then I went away to patrol the streets of hell
She stayed in Kitchener, with her family keeping well

I stumbled and crawled through a number of life's tests
I challenged them back, but booze was my best

"You gotta slow things down," she used to always say
"If you don't, you may end up leaving us tragically one day"

Gary Rubie and Henk Rubie

I paid no heed to her words of warning
And for many years I suffered with mourning

The years flew by like minutes on the clock
When I finally hit my bottom, at my door was a knock

It was my big sister; she picked me off the floor and wiped away my tears
She got me cleaned up and threw out my beers

She never judged, knew I lived my own hell, then she gave me extra love
Since I couldn't love myself, she watched over me like a dove

I finally got well, and she stood by my side
Other so-called friends got embarrassed, went to hide

Today she's the glue that keeps the family together
I owe my big sister my life for helping me face the stormy weather

Out On A Cliff

FRANK

WHEN MY FIST CLENCHES, CRACK IT OPEN,
BEFORE I USE IT AND LOSE MY COOL.

—THE WHO, "BEHIND BLUE EYES"

You got run down as the daylight set
Almost ended your life, not dying yet

A ten-speed simply is no match for a truck
What was he thinking? Didn't he see you? What the fuck

You flew through the air, then crumbled to the ground
A shattered leg, jaw, bike, and life is what they found

The pain that followed, I couldn't comprehend
How will they fix you? How will you mend?

Many calls were made; I was the one they got
"We need permission to operate." Go ahead, give it your best shot

I didn't even change clothes, travelled five cities in a blink
Then at the hospital we rallied; no one knew what to think

Several doctors worked on you together, then you went to ICU
What would be the outcome? We can't help; what can we do?

Out On A Cliff

More surgeries would follow; the head injury took its toll
Grade 14, a few "U. of Goo" credits; years slipped by after you enrolled

The road to recovery would be long and slow
How long would it take? Even you didn't know

They rebuilt your leg; the bone wouldn't take
So they put in the hardware for again it would break

You woke up during surgery, amazing you didn't come undone
You had to lie there and bear it; you couldn't get up and run

When the jaw was unwired, you got new pearly whites
But the pain in your arm kept you up most nights

The fingers wouldn't move; you went under the knife again
They did a nerve transplant, then you found your Zen

You studied the mind and learned how to control your pain
When you faced great adversity, it's amazing the insight you gained

GARY RUBIE AND HENK RUBIE

As for the man responsible for almost taking your life
I was gonna hunt him down, cut him up with a knife

You never got resentful and moved on with your life
You got a job, had a family, and took on a wife

So, little brother, this you need to know
You saved my life, and I never told you so

You inspired in me survival, to never surrender to the pain
It helped me survive; my pain was different, yet the same

I thank the great Eagle Spirit for leaving you here
I'm sure that if he'd taken you away, I'd have drowned in the beer

I'll never forget the statement that was made on a tequila whim
"You can break a Rubie's bones, but you can never kill him."

A brother's bond can never be broken.
Friends for good . . . Partners forever . . . Tough guys for life.

Out On A Cliff

Gary Rubie and Henk Rubie

THE TOWERS TAKE TWO

Many years ago, you did time with me
We had a lot of fun; you lived by the left sea

You had a few years on me, lived a life of plenty
But I was a cop and lived the life of twenty

I was quickly attracted, the lure of the actress
Watched you on the set, then spent time on the mattress

We partied a little, and you showed me LA
Talked about marriage, but I couldn't stay

Many years went by; I often wondered how you were
But we lived different lives; years went by like a blur

Then I heard that you moved and you left the West Coast
Writing plays in New York, where you could hide like a ghost

You had a penchant for cops, and you ran into John
It was a match made in heaven; this guy wasn't a con

You got engaged and planned a new life
Then tragedy struck; you weren't to be his wife

The planes crashed into both, and they started to burn
It was a matter of time, the point of no return

John turned left when he should have turned right
He died that day in that burial site

They called it Ground Zero; it was horrible to see
The tragedy took John and then Debra-Lee

Her pain was so great; the bottle took it away
Then her life was cut short; with us she didn't stay

Out On A Cliff

It breaks my heart to know that you're actually gone
I didn't say good-bye; we didn't talk for so long

I wish there was something, just anything I could've done
But I know that you died of a broken heart under the sun

September 11, 2001
So many lives changed, so many lives gone

We can't turn the clocks back and make it all right
My friend is now gone; she's slipped into the night

BIG YELLOW

Went to the Eiffel Tower; all I could see was you
Hair was blond, eyes were blue

Got a gold ring for both our left hands
Got to get back together, gotta make amends

I miss you so much, can't stand the pain
Those feelings keep rolling around in my brain

'Cuz you and I should have taken that trip
Many years ago, but I just couldn't get a grip

I miss you so bad that my heart—it could break
My god, I can't believe I made this mistake

So many years ago, I let you fly
All I can do today is just sit back and cry

I wish you were here; I wouldn't let you go
But I blew it back then, a long time ago

I think of you often; you're deep in my head
I dream of the day I'll hold you close in my bed

But dreams won't get you back into my life
Because for now, you are someone else's wife

So I say it again, I'm so sorry for the scars
When I promised you the earth, the moon, and the stars

Taken this trip alone . . .

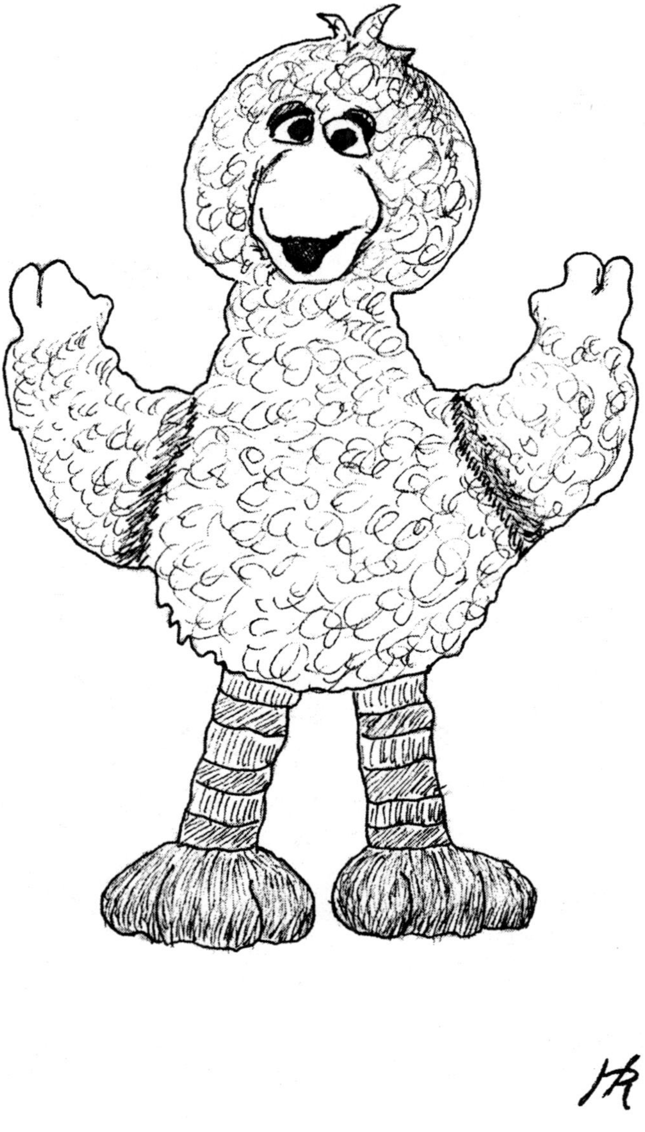

FOREVER IN MY HEART

It started on the dance floor
A very long time ago
Where would it take us?
How far could we go?

There was so much passion
But nothing in between
I couldn't find the balance
So you had to leave

We created a life
And I vowed mine forever
But the house we had built
Just couldn't storm the weather

You made a hard choice
The decision wasn't mine
You knew what you had to do
Things would be just fine

You were stronger than I
My pain had just begun
Had to travel much darkness
Before I would see sun

So the years went by
And time wasn't so kind
Rarely did a day pass
When you weren't on my mind

A couple of chance meetings
We had along the way
But the sadness grew in my heart
'Cuz I knew you couldn't stay

Out On A Cliff

So we'd hug and we'd kiss
And finally we would part
How much had we missed?
Could I make a new start?

And with each new beginning
I would try hard to forget
But I just wasn't winning
She'd come back to me yet

Many more years went by
And though only a few pictures remained
Fond memories of those happy eyes
The deep love in my heart never changed

So the thoughts grew stronger
Of a love I had lost
Then one day a phone call
Was this done by the boss?

So now I need to tell you
My dear old friend
I gave you my heart
Until the very end

Wherever you go
Whatever you do
What you need to know
I'll wait forever for you

Something this strong
The feelings remain
No man, woman, or child
Could get in the way

So live your life out in peace
And be true to what you built
I just need you to know this
Without sadness or guilt

For this was chosen for me
This is the path I'm to take
Living clean and with serenity
Being here for you if you break

So I make you one last promise
That if you stumble and fall
I'll be right there to pick you up
Children and all

For there will be no more sadness
No more flying away
If your house ever blows down
I'll be back with you to stay

And then you will feel me
And I will feel you
And we shall never, ever part
Until our days are through

It started on the dance floor
A very long time ago
Where will it take us?
How far can we go?

Or . . .

Will you become
One of the five people I meet in heaven?

Out On A Cliff

THE END

It started out just as a dream
Was gonna be this way forever
Life ain't always what it seems
Didn't see the stormy weather

Was a clear and sunny start
Then the leaves, they started to change
I gave it all; I gave her my heart
Both our lives got rearranged

When the snow began to fall
I lit a fire so we wouldn't be cold
She wanted more; she wanted it all
This storm was getting old

I had to choose a different way
But will the little angels survive?
The toughest decision I had to make
How long could I stay alive?

When the snow began to melt
And the sun began to shine
The old feelings I once felt
Were gone till the end of time

THE GRAND CANYON

Walked in together; she couldn't stay
Had to get the kids later on that day
It took longer than planned; something wasn't quite right
Didn't know what; it was outta my sight

They kept me for hours
What had gone wrong?
Finally went to my room
The night seemed long

Started to drift
"Leafs" on the tube
Morphine on a drip
I started to lose

Woke up in pain
Where had I been?
Out on a cliff
Was it all a bad dream?

Two weeks in hell
Sent up to the ward
Gave up on life
No time to get bored

The body started to heal
The pain was a real strain
But I just couldn't fight
What went on in my brain

He took me to hell
Then let me return
I just wasn't well
My heart got burned

Stayed out on the cliff
Things just got worse
Pills, booze, cocaine, and spliff
Someone just call the hearse

Out On A Cliff

Then I started to heal
The pain was still there
Didn't know what to feel
Do I really care?

I decided to live
Took back my own life
But the cost was so great
My sweet kids and my wife

So today I'm alive
Without any rift
Living each day
As though it were a gift

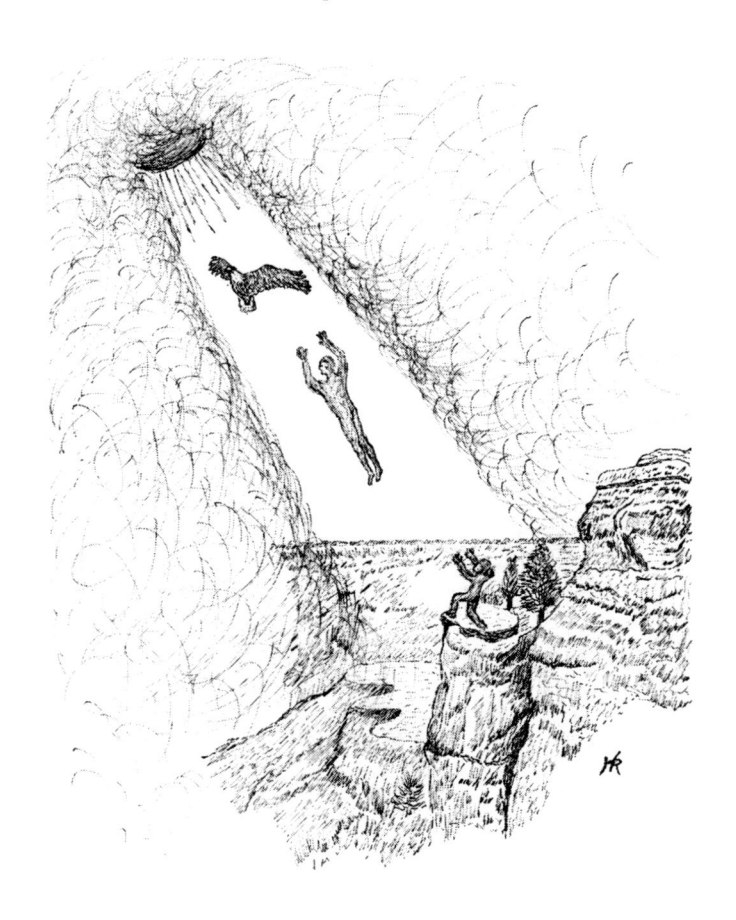

A MEMORY

Walked down the beach, seen the old spot
Was it all out of reach, should I take another shot?

Time goes by quickly; it never stands still
We keep growing older; am I over the hill?

We've both taken different roads
She went high; I went low

Can't quit this feeling, like something's still there
Do I go back to her or just step back and glare?

Get a grip, you fool; this isn't the end
Pull it together right now; you're on the mend

We fixed you up good, made everything tight
Is it the end of world, is everything all right?

Let's keep it together; life's like that sometimes
You've walked alone before, without the poor-me whines

It's just a memory now; yesterday is over
Your luck has changed; hold on to the clover

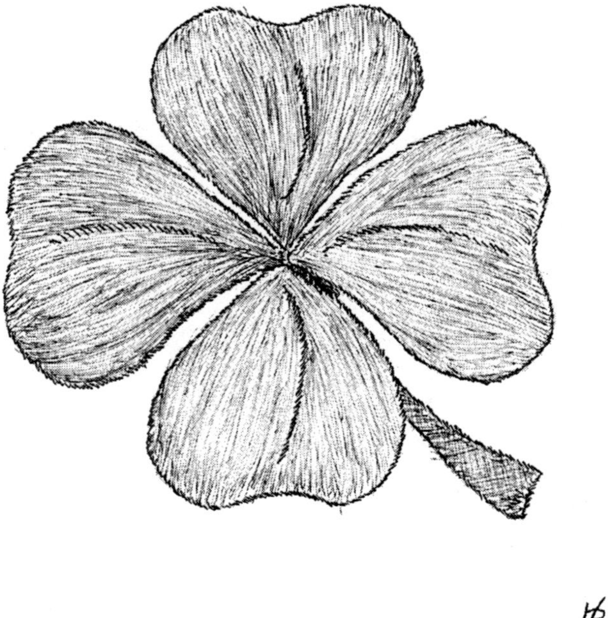

THE TIES THAT BIND

I was so excited when the water broke
It was a long nine months; that's no joke

You were my first; I can never forget
I was finally gonna be a father; was I ready yet?

A long night of labor, then out you came
Long and lean with twenty digits; we even had your name

I cut the cord, and the bond was made then
When I held you the first time, it was surreal and Zen

I kissed your little forehead; you had a certain smell
It's a smell you never forget, that only a parent can tell

Babies smell new, clean, and fresh; they are delicate as a butterfly
And like a butterfly, they grow and explore, find their place in life, then fly

We brought you home, and time went by
Your mom went back to work, and it was my turn to try

So back to work she went, and I received approval to stay home
It was the most special time I ever spent with anyone alone

The bond got so strong that no one could break it
I credit the time we spent home alone is what made it

A few years have slipped behind us, and we've grown
You're a young lady now, coming into your own

But what I still see when I look in your eyes
Is the sweet little girl with whom I made ties

Out On A Cliff

BABY BLUE

Your mother screamed, "My water's broke
C'mon, Gary, this ain't no joke"

But a strange thing happened; I got all weird
Started making the beds, cleaned up, shaved my beard

"Hurry up now," your mother said
"She's popping out, I can feel her head"

We got in the car, and I made one last stop
Asked your aunt for advice; she said, "Get going, you nutty cop"

We were a hundred kilometers from hospital to home
I drove a "buck sixty," timed contractions, used the phone

While I was checking your mom in, she fell to the floor
"Hurry up, call the doctor, she can't wait anymore"

You almost arrived before the doctor came
We were blown away by the color of your mane

White-blond hair, pale skin, and baby blue eyes
You came to this planet with the loudest cries

I used to watch you sleep, watch your chest go up and down
Watch you make funny faces, watch you smile and frown

Your sister was quiet, but you had an edge
You could run through the drywall, jump over the hedge

So you're older now, but the memories live on
I think of them each time I see my six foot blonde

She's got good genes; now she's strong and lean
I love my Baby Blue; she's a laughing machine

Out On A Cliff

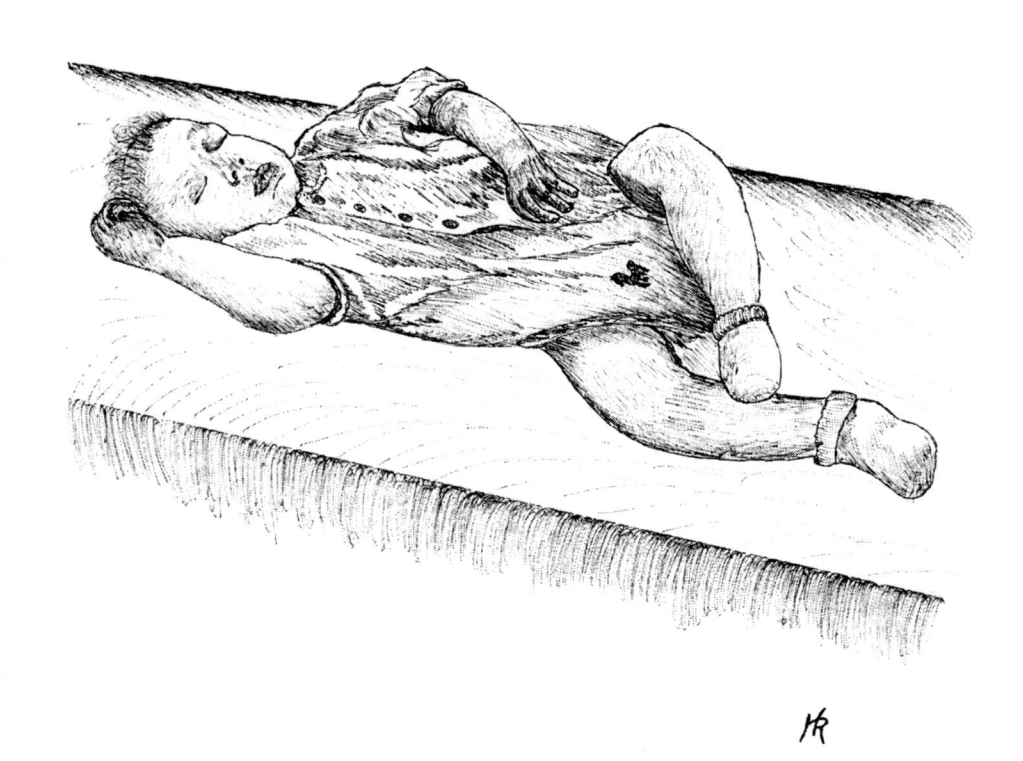

Gary Rubie and Henk Rubie

THE NIKKI POEM

She was born on May 30, 1998
For the first four months, cried every night straight

We bought a new house that had central air
Realized her problem was having wet hair

She was fussy at first, hated the heat
Had a period of adjustment, then turned very sweet

Under the sweetness, the little devil lurked
Had her little dark side, mischievous and perked

We started to call her Taz, like the Tasmanian devil
Started to get into trouble, and in the mischief, she'd revel

She was albino blond and had eyes of blue
She was tall, long, and lean; man, she really grew

Her older sister had dark hair, skin, and eyes
Nikki was different as the morning and night skies

When she learned to talk, she began to tell jokes
A comedian in school and in front of her folks

When she was six, I moved out of the house
For a while she was affected and became quiet as a mouse

Her sister took it worse and wanted to come to her dad
Nikki was a mommy's girl, so she never seemed sad

Both girls witnessed drinking, yelling, and fighting
As they grew older, the drama became exciting

Masters of manipulation, both seemed to develop the skill
Pushing certain buttons and painful utterances gave them both a thrill

For a year the oldest was with me, and Nikki with her mom
It all changed this year, one week off, one week on

This keeps the girls together, even though they travel to different schools
A week at Mom's and a week at Dad's they follow the same rules

She's quite a young girl; they really grow up quick
My Nikki and I have really started to click

TAZ

Gary Rubie and Henk Rubie

GYPSY ON THE DRIP

It was the worst of the times
It was the best of times[1]

I am everything . . . I am nothing . . .[2]

She believed in him,
He believed in her[3]

The boat left the dock
The water was so still
She was in a lock
Did they have the will?

Time runs a race
Life is the training ground
Sometimes it's hard to pace
It passes like the speed of sound

Chasing down each sunset
Watching every wave
Programmed by a system
Turning into a slave

The good die young
There's no rhyme or reason
We all sing different songs
Season after season

Live fast and play hard
Time will pass; deal another card

---

[1] Dickens
[2] Unknown
[3] Unknown

Out On A Cliff

A game of survival
Chasing the dream
Then upon arrival
It's just not what it seems

The stakes were high
We played for keeps
Was it all just a lie?
Everyone's a creep

So you got what you worked for
And now you pay the price
You made the choice to go through that door
And in the end, it wasn't that nice

Sacrifices that you made
For this long loyal career
A woman fighting in a man's game
You gave it a lifetime, year after year

We stopped for tea
Along the way
But I drank coffee
Maybe another day

A surprise visit after testing recruits
Just maybe for a while we'll wear the same boots

The snow was falling that November night
Floyd was playing; it felt just right

A trip soon followed to the coral-colored sea
It was a helluva time, just you and me

We discovered the Tiki in the Texas sun
It was heaven on earth; that trip was fun

Then all of a sudden, things started to change
Where was I living? Missed my home on the range

How do I stop this? I can't quit boozing
My life is ending; I think I'm losing

She drove me to the door and left me at the street
I'd have to return alone if this thing I would beat

There'll be lots of heartache; it's a terrible blow
But I knew in my heart that I just had to go

I fell into the hole just one more time
But when I climbed out, things were just fine

So time went by, and we didn't drink tea
She taught me to love; I finally loved me

Then I got the bad phone call; God, say it ain't true
How much time is left, what the hell can I do?

Our journey has taught her to live one day at a time
And together we pray that it will all be fine

So now she's hooked up to the drip every day
How much is in the bag, how long will she stay?

And for today, I have hope for my friend
The frizzy-haired gypsy, I'll love her till the end

Out On A Cliff

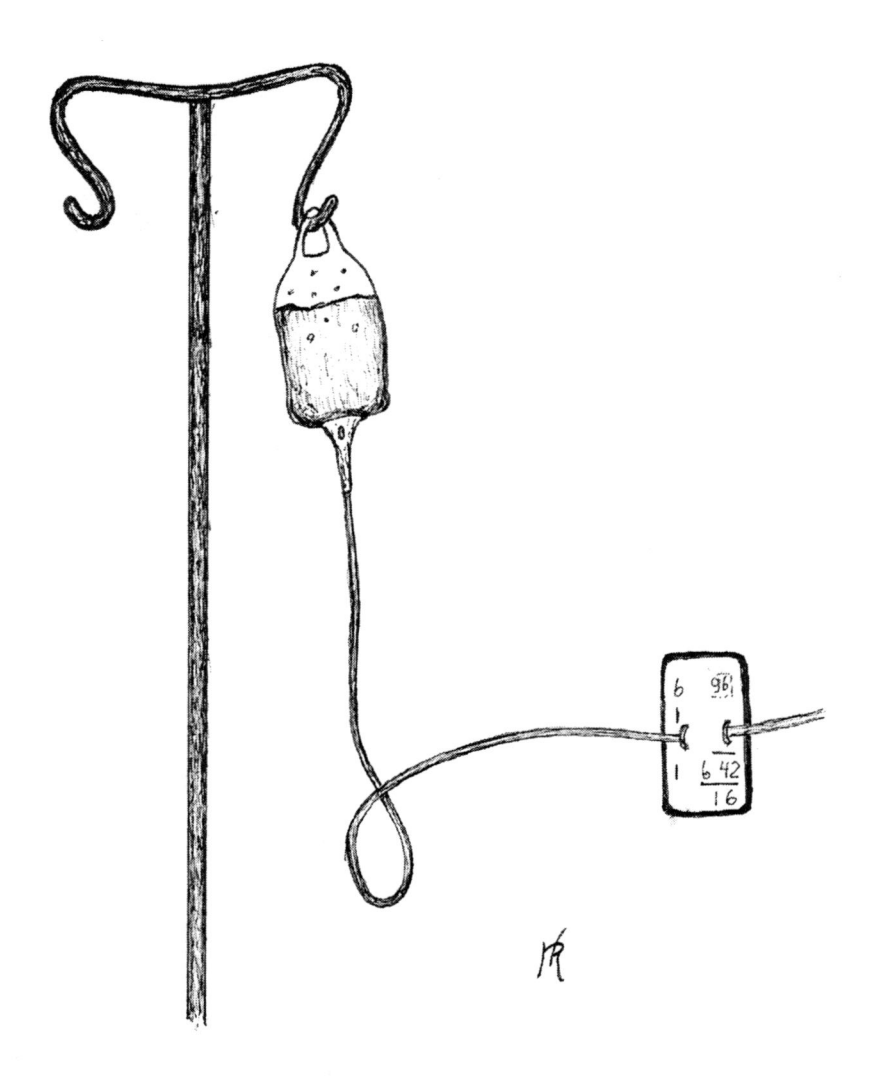

GOOD-BYE, MY FRIEND

You gave everyone you touched
Unconditional love

So where else could you be
But in heaven above?

God gives wings
To his angels at the gate

But for some strange reason,
With you, he didn't wait

For you earned your wings
Long before you left earth

Day after day,
You showed everyone your worth

So there's no more pain
No more burdens to bear

You're dancing with the angels
And a new head of hair

As each day passes,
The sadness will subside

And your loving memory
Will live forever inside

With these hands
I give you my heart and my loyalty

GOODBYE
MY FRIEND
JUNE 28 1966 - APR 25, 2008
FOREVER IN OUR HEARTS
HR

R 2 CC

Got to the EX, dropped off my bike
Three thousand in line; this would be a big hike

What have I done, will I finish this ride?
If my leg didn't hold up, I'd go on ego and pride

I started this journey when she first got sick
But time wasn't kind; the darkness was thick

I hadn't trained hard enough; four months took their toll
Emotions ran high when I got to the poll

Three thousand together, each had their own cause
But they all believed in victory; no one saw this as a loss

The day was incredible; it ended so high
When the music was over, saw my friend in the sky

Tent City lay quiet under the stars of the night
Just one more day to go, and all would be right

It hurt to get on that old bike the very next day
But the one-legged rider would show me the way

They raised fourteen million on that two-day event
Every cent donated was money well spent

So we have to keep fighting to find answers—a cure
When this will happen, none of us is really sure

But the beast we are fightin' might not be the disease
We may have to assassinate the big corporate "head cheese"

So for now I'll keep faith and turn over the wheel
Put my trust into God, for I know he will heal

Out On A Cliff

SKITTER-BUG

Where did you go, you old skitter-bug?
I heard that they found you facedown on the rug

How did it happen, did your heart give out?
Did it render you lame, couldn't you stand up and shout?

Or maybe you planned it to all end this way
Knowing full well they'd come in on Monday

But time will tell, toxicology will show
What really happened why you had to go.

I can't make sense of the things that you said
But it's clear to me now that you'd rather be dead

Unusual behavior for the past ten days
It was in your eyes; it was in your gaze

The eyes that used to sparkle and shine with life
Became dark as tombstones holding a knife

Unanswered questions that were making me nuts
For twenty-fours, I hated your guts

I just can't imagine how your son must feel
But from my daughter's eyes, the pain is real

So for now I say thank you for the time that we shared
'Cuz I know that you loved me; you showed me you cared

You introduced me to God, the one that rules all
You said if I believed, I wouldn't stumble and fall

You had more faith than any man I had seen
We shared with each other what we did, where we'd been

You showed me the prophet and gave me strength to go on
Now I journey alone because you are gone

Out On A Cliff

Gary Rubie and Henk Rubie

THE PORCH

I sit here alone, up high on my porch
Looking at the construction, someone give me a torch

This town's growing fast, can't keep up with the pace
All kinds of new faces, many different kinds of race

The face was pale; now it's got lots of color
Took a different shape, seemed the town went to the cellar

So number one finally decided she wanted to move in
Bought a semi in the south, dumped out my gin

And each night she kisses me and says "I love you"
I spend time on my porch just checkin' the view

The streets have no names
The houses all look the same

The people don't have faces
Their shoes all have the same laces

All families have two jobs
They live their lives like slobs

Like characters in a bad movie
They all think they're so groovy

And each night I wonder, did I make the right choice?
Each morning I'm reminded by that sweet young voice

Oh, a challenge it's been since she first came aboard
Have to check all I do with my good friend the Lord

Guess I shouldn't sit up here and judge
I can't afford to hold on to a grudge

And when deep down I feel like it's all gone mad
I'm grateful it's not the same as the crazy life I once had

Out On A Cliff

GARY RUBIE AND HENK RUBIE

ME AND MY GIRL

It doesn't matter how hard I try
If I shed a few tears or outright cry

You refuse to listen to the voice of reason
We're drifting apart for more than a season

The apple doesn't fall too far from the tree
I wish you understand and see what I see

Your tongue is starting to slash my skin
Hurting my emotions, wearing me thin

So for now I must take a step back
Feel I'm being tested; I feel under attack

Need to create distance, move away from the pain
You continue to challenge me again and again

This is the toughest decision I've had to make
I know you don't understand what's at stake

All that I want is a calm happy life
Even if that means taking on a new wife

So please understand, I'm not choosing sides
It was a matter of time before our worlds collide

Use this time wisely, and don't hold a grudge
Remember that none of us have the right to judge

And I will always love you from the bottom of my heart
Until the last day that God tears us apart

OUT ON A CLIFF

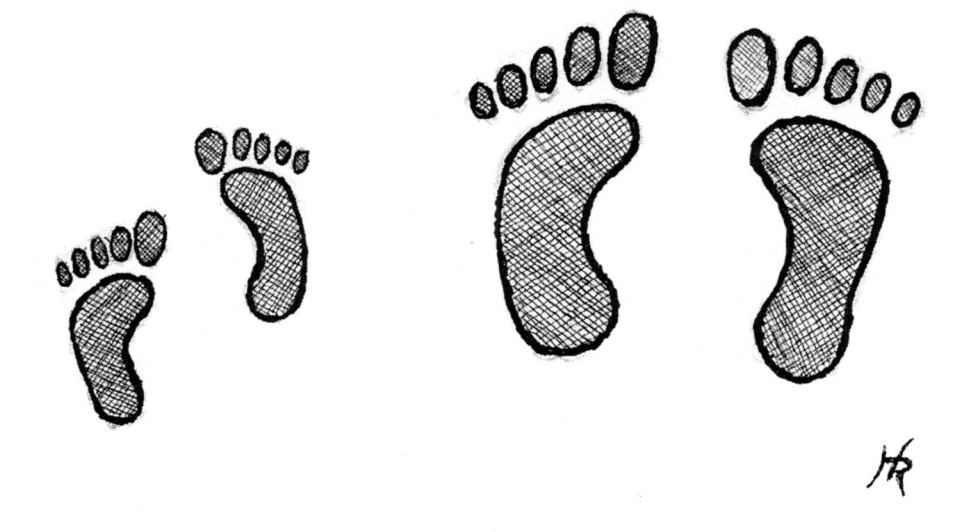

UNDERSTANDING

I know you're frustrated, angry, and sad
But I'm doing my best to be a good dad

You're not giving me a chance to explain my decisions
To share my future, my dreams, my visions

You tell me that I'm a shitty father
You swear at me, punk me, tell me to not bother

I don't understand what you and your sister feel
'Cuz my dad and mom never welshed on their deal

They stayed together for over fifty years
Your mother and I caused you girls lots of tears

I could never find the words that would make amends
Make you both feel better for bringing my marriage to an end

It was never my intention to hurt you girls
If I could take it all back, you'd both wear pearls

But yesterday is gone with the people that were in it
I have to move my life forward now; I just can't quit

I don't know what I'd say if my dad or mom remarried
It's what I've chosen for me because my past has been buried

The decisions I make are not meant to hurt you
I just want you to be happy and not feel blue

I cannot force you to feel this way
You treating me poorly will not make me sway

You can accept the decision that I've chosen to make
Or keep trying to punish me, saying I made a mistake

Telling me that at fourteen, you are smarter than me
Calling me an addict and slighting me with glee

Out On A Cliff

You won't change my decision, won't change my mind
You may push me away and continue to be unkind

But you'll always be my baby, and I will love you to the end
No matter the decision you make, no matter if you bend

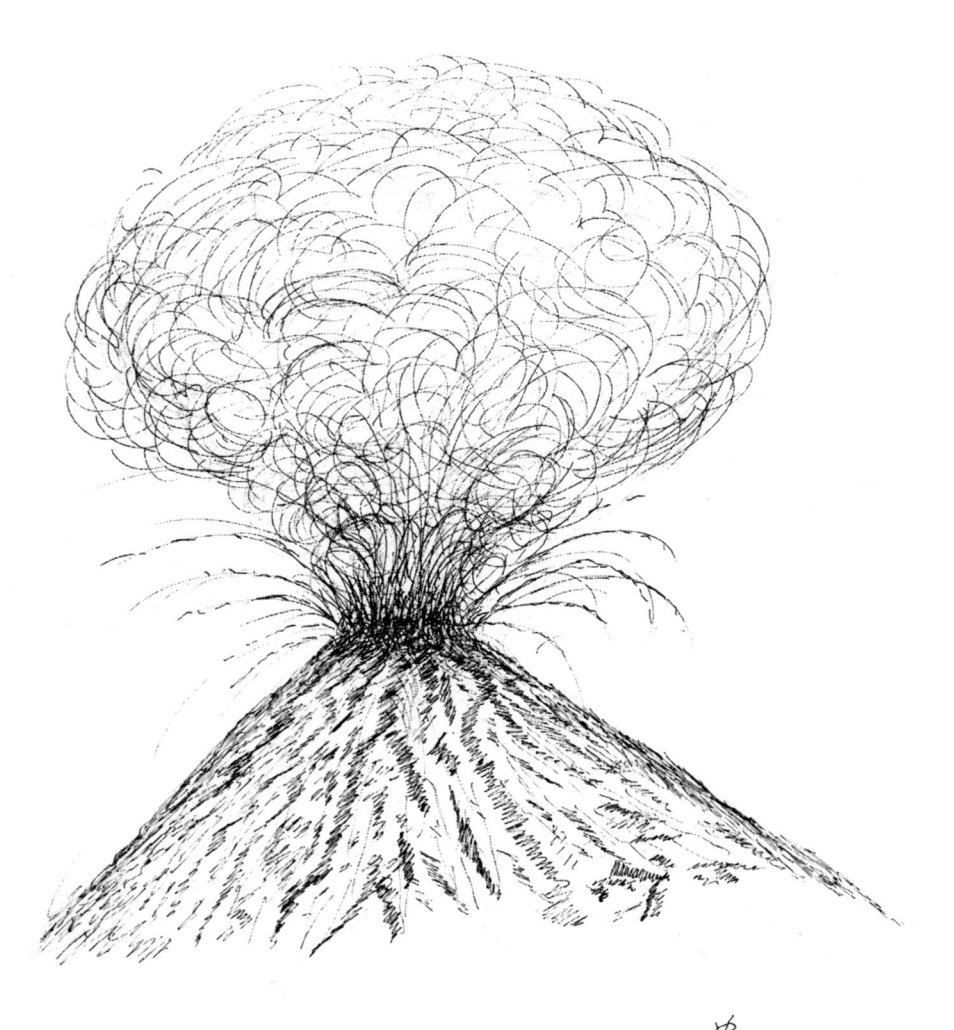

Gary Rubie and Henk Rubie

WHEN YOU . . . I FEEL . . . I NEED . . .

I can't explain the action you took
When you . . . I feel . . . I need

It doesn't matter who threw the first hook
When you . . . I feel . . . I need . . .

The pebble has grown the size of a boulder
When you . . . I feel . . . I need . . .

Sharp words were said; sudden action took over
When you . . . I feel . . . I need . . .

Never talked things through, I knew what was best
When you . . . I feel . . . I need . . .

My heart has been shattered, ripped out of my chest
When you . . . I feel . . . I need . . .

I won't back down; I've done nothing wrong
When you . . . I feel . . . I need . . .

You played your mom; now you've strung me along
When you . . . I feel . . . I need . . .

Someday you both will see the results
When you . . . I feel . . . I need . . .

Of the action you took, without a consult
When you . . . I feel . . . I need . . .

But by then it may be a little too late
When you . . . I feel . . . I need . . .

Time will slip away the longer you wait
When you . . . I feel . . . I need . . .

It's an empty feeling, won't go away
When you . . . I feel . . . I need . . .

Out On A Cliff

You'll always be my kids, no matter what you say
When you . . . I feel . . . I need . . .

It doesn't matter how this nightmare ends
When you . . . I feel . . . I need . . .

Remember you may never be able to make amends
When you . . . I feel . . . I need . . .

ANGEL FROM THE A&P—CHAPTER 1

Shopping for turkey was on Christmas Eve
Head wasn't right, body wanted to heave

And then I'd seen the angel, her glow had hurt my eyes
Sweet as a child in a manger; felt a weakness in my thighs

I went and spoke to the angel; her voice was peace and love
How on earth could she not be? She was sent from heaven above

We spoke for over an hour; it was like time was standing still
But what was the hidden message, was she to help me up the hill?

So who sent the angel for me? Would she take me, or would she guide?
I'm not ready to go to heaven yet, so we go together on the ride

We met again days later; I accepted that she's actually real
The whole thing wasn't a dream; I would have to tell her how I feel

So I shared some of my darkness; never once did she judge
This angel sent from heaven; I may let go and actually *love*

I want to get to know her; I want her to know all of me
For if that doesn't happen first, this relationship will never be

So I won't run when I'm feeling the emotions, not leaving just because
I can never forget that Christmas Eve when an angel was sent from above

ANGEL FROM THE A&P—CHAPTER 2

So a week's gone by, and we've done some time
The many hours we've spent far beyond just fine

She listens so closely, hears everything I say
I have to sometimes wonder, will she be here to stay?

She is pure in her intention; her love seems so real
When I wrap my arms around her, can't hide what I feel

So I told her that I loved her, seemed to happen so fast
Do you believe in fate, baby? Do you think this will last?

The feelings overwhelm me, my heart races—can't stop
Whenever you are near me, I crown the mountaintop

But I won't fight those feelings; I let them go once before
There's nothing more painful than letting true love walk out the door

Two glorious nights behind us, the passion continues to grow
I just couldn't imagine that this could possibly slow

So I sit alone in the hotel room, Mother Nature all around
Up here to get myself grounded, so grateful for what I'd found

But the real test lies ahead, for in two days I fly away
Will she be waiting for her love to return, or will she turn and walk away?

My gut says she'll be waiting, and for eight days my heart will burst
And when I walk off that jumbo jet, I know I'll taste her thirst

'Cuz distance makes the heart grow fonder, makes us wish we'd never gone
So from here on in when I take a trip, my baby will come along

ANGEL FROM THE A&P—CHAPTER 3

A month has passed; we have become one
She was waiting for me when I returned from the sun

Distance made the heart grow fonder, our love stronger than before
I know we won't flounder; she's not walking out the door

We're together every day, so hard to be apart
She's in my every fiber, has a rope around my heart

So she took a week's vacation; we're together every day
I love my angel from the A&P in every imaginable way

She gives me certain calmness I haven't seen for years
Obsession to use was lifted, not craving substances and beers

We talk for endless hours, fall asleep in each other's arms
Nothing can pull us apart, no earthquake, no fire alarms

And when we awake each morning, there's a glow around her eyes
Such genuine love between us, nothing pretentious, no disguise

So we talk about our future, and what we both agree
That we need to be together, I with her and she with me

The excitement fills my heart, feelings I can't contain
Emotions of joy and love flow from my heart up to my brain

I want the world to know about my newfound love
I want to scream from a mountaintop that an angel flew down from above

One thing is certain, I cannot tell a lie
Gonna be with her forever until the day I die

ANGEL FROM THE A&P—CHAPTER 4

Well, I had to go away to get myself well
My angel walked beside me through the gates of hell

Every Friday she got me; every Sunday she took me back
This wasn't a joke; I had to get myself on track

It was a terrible hurdle to have to jump
I had to finish it all, or I'd end up a hump

The angel never wavered from start to finish
And our relationship kept growing; it didn't diminish

There were happy greetings and tearful good-byes
It was a part of the process; together we were growing wise

When the end finally came, I'd been transformed
The tears were all gone, and the weather had warmed

We had a great summer, growing closer each day
It was becoming real clear that we were both here to stay

My angel walked beside me through every dark hour
She taught me a lesson that together we had strength and power

So I bought her a ring, said, "Let's finish this trip"
Never felt a love this deep; she had me in her grip

We went to the water, and I dropped to one knee
She said yes right away; we were both filled with glee

Decided we would visit the Eiffel Tower
Share our vows in Europe, that will be our hour

We decided to do the same over here
To have our kids involved, make the ceremony sincere

Becoming Cathy's husband is like marrying my best friend
We're gonna grow old together, gonna love her to the end

Gary Rubie and Henk Rubie

YOU TAUGHT ME

We travelled the road together, through the darkness and the light
We've had our share of struggles; we even had the odd fight

But you taught me great lessons, lessons of love
You taught me to love me and seek help from above

You taught me to forgive and to not hold a grudge
You showed me how to forgive myself and not wallow in the sludge

You taught me that crying doesn't weaken a man
You said it was okay, that if I need to, I can

You taught me how to be a parent, the fine line between father and friend
You taught me to be firm, not to buckle, not to bend

You taught me to be genuine and honest with all
You said you saw it in my writings; they were once shallow and small

You taught me to be patient and not to lose self-control
Your patience is a like a saint's, digging me out of every hole

You have become a part of me, the better part, I will say
You've given me reason to live my life, to carry on and stay

I became a very lonely man, always feeling insecure
With you in my life, the loneliness left, and I've never felt so sure

I begged for a message from high above that lonely Christmas night
You were placed intentionally in my path so I could see the light

My life today is anything but darkness, and that is because of you
For you have taught me to practice faith and patience, and all my dreams
have come true

We travelled the road together, through the darkness and the light
We've had our share of struggles; we even had the odd fight

Out On A Cliff

ANOTHER RELATIONSHIP

The walk in the park became a run through hell
When you jump in quick, it's hard to tell

Everyone behaves in a certain way
Their actions determine if they want you to stay

Some actions are real; some actions are fake
Some gardens you pull weeds; others you rake

You wear your heart on your sleeve, believe transparency is best
Some will prey on your weakness; some will sleep in your nest

So whatever your choice, wherever you run
Always remember, not everyone is fun

One thing's for sure, they take a lot of work
But you still won't know if you're with a real jerk

'Cuz every once in a while, you get whacked between the eyes
Have they been up-front, or were you fed shit and lies?

No matter how it ends, you had family involved
As each conflict passes, is it ever resolved?

Pointing a finger is a dirty, sleazy game
To some that comes easy; just don't mention their name

So the walk through the park became a run through hell
Makes you wish upon a star that this time it went well

Out On A Cliff

THE SUNSET

A man lives his life that's long and full
There are many struggles; there is push and pull

A man's life isn't judged by his final net worth
His life is defined by the good he did on earth

He spends forty-five years providing for others
His work ethic came from his father and mother

When he cleaned up his tools and entered the golden years
He earned every sunset and a couple'a beers

For the man knows when he reflects in the mirror
That the golden years have made his life much clearer

A man has many friends during his entire life's stride
But none are as loyal as the dog by his side

He's shared his darkest secrets and told him many tales
But his friend never judged; he listened intently and wagged his tail

Now as the final sunset gets closer each day
The loyalty between dog and man grew stronger without sway

When the day ends and the final sunset goes down
The last one standing doesn't know how he can go on

For the last sunset took his best friend away
While a piece of the one living left with his friend that day

Out On A Cliff

Gary Rubie and Henk Rubie

ANGEL FROM THE A&P—FINAL CHAPTER

I couldn't undo what I had done
The seed was planted deep
It used to be that we had such fun
But now I just can't sleep

It's no ones fault it ended this way
We simply grew apart
You were in my head, you were in my bed
You occupied my heart

They say that people are placed in your life
At precisely the right time
You entered mine when it was full of strife
And together we did climb

We began this journey against all odds
No one thought it would survive
You followed me up to mountaintops
Stood beside me while I was barely alive

It's a difficult emotion to try and replace
When someone loses hope
Neither of us realized the depth of your loss
Neither knew the scope

I see it every time I look into your eyes
I can hear it in your voice
I told you often to turn and run
I said you had a choice

You chose to stay, and as time went on
We began wearing different coats
Our fights and spats became a war
Words turned to switchblades slashing at our throats

There's just been too much chaos
I want it all to stop
I can't explain, but it's making me insane
My world is spinning like a top

Out On A Cliff

People come into your life
For a reason, a season, a lifetime
You've been my brightest season so far
For a while, you were my lifeline

It's not healthy now for either of us
You need to take back your life
You weren't meant to be my hostage
You were supposed to be my wife

It breaks my heart to say good-bye
It's just how it's got to be
Maybe in another season
You'll come back to my family tree

The End

POLICING

MY FIRST YEAR

August 27, 1984
Mom stood crying for me at the back door

Did the drive to Brampton, got there late
Didn't know about morning traffic, arrived at twenty past eight

Not a good way to start a policing career
Little did I know, it would be a really hard year

I was oblivious to the madness and chaos going on
A Peel cop was murdered by a longtime con

There were press and cameras all around the station
I just didn't understand the magnitude of the situation

Three days passed, then they honored our fallen cop
Over seven thousand attended; this funeral was over the top

Cops from Canada and the United States converged in Brampton
It was a total mob scene, like a concert by Peter Frampton

Couldn't believe what I saw, cops trading their shirts and hats
Driving cruisers while drinking liquor, and everyone was smashed

Memorial Gardens Arena hosted the party, with its free food and bar
It must have been an incredible sight for people watching from afar

I went to more funerals that first year of different murdered cops
And as quickly as the killings started, they suddenly just stopped

So that was the experience of my first year
Filled me with anxiety, filled me with fear

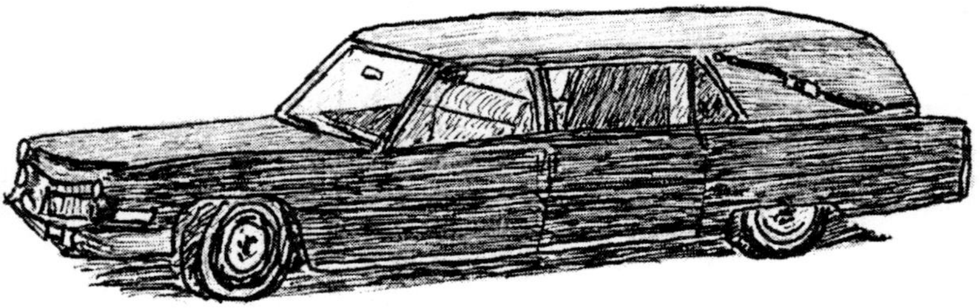

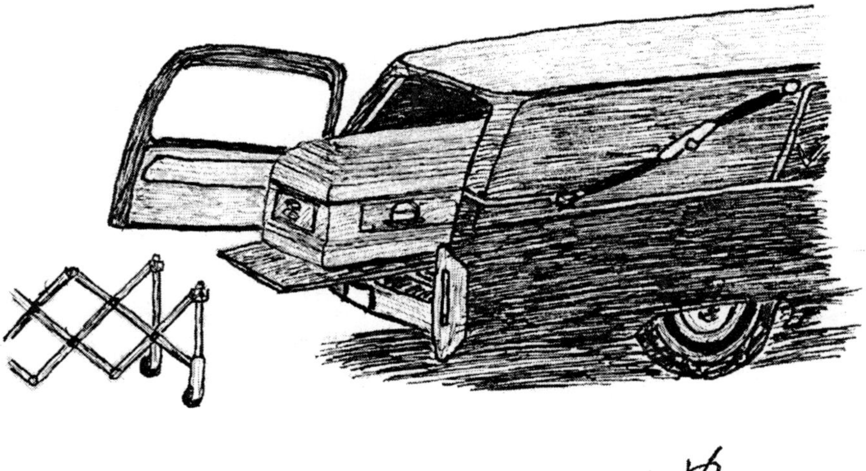

Gary Rubie and Henk Rubie

TOOLS OF MY TRADE

They sent me away to study for hours
They gave me a badge and a bag full of powers

To the college of knowledge in a little small town
Made us march like toy soldiers, but I felt like a clown

They had a bar on the campus, cheap beer, pickled eggs
Used to sit there at night till I felt rubber in my legs

I hated that place and the power they had
They got in my cage, nearly drove me mad

Yes sir, no sir, go polish your leather
Now go run outside, don't give a shit about the weather

And when you are done, drop down and give me twenty
Look straight ahead, boy, I ain't your honey

I hated that place; they thought they built men
I would have had more fun doin' a deuce in the pen

When I got my BA, they sent me to Peel
I was pushin' a yellow, sat alone behind the wheel

It was there that I learned to walk the thin blue line
I was taken to places so unreal, I lost time

The time had begun to slip quickly away
Felt I was losing a year for each day

It's a hard price to pay when you're working the street
But you always protected the people on your beat

And as a long thirty years slowly comes to a close
You pray you cross the line, don't get buried under a rose

So you earned your ring, take a bow, take a lap
And forget the last thirty years and all of its crap

Out On A Cliff

SCOTTY

No one's certain how the end really came
One pull of the trigger put a bullet through his brain

He was my partner, he was my friend
Why did it have to come to an end?

In the black of the night,
A search turned into a fight

One sucker punch, and he's down on the ground
.38 in the wrong hand, one chamber, one round

He pulled the trigger and changed fate forever
So many lives ripped apart, never to be together

Wife lost her husband; kids lost their dad
A city in mourning, each one of us sad

Then we laid him to rest in that final place
The government sat in the front row; what a disgrace

A memory, a dream, all gone to the past
Pain that lasts a lifetime, like shards of shattered glass

So the heat got turned up to capture Satan's slave
Detectives were told of a secret shallow grave

The "skell" he was there, but the trophy was lost,
We will search a lifetime for its return at any cost

Out On A Cliff

NIGHTS

You sent me out to work in the dark
I walked the downtown alleys and the city park

It wasn't easy being a rookie on the streets
I patrolled in a car and walked the beat

I had to shake down the bad guys in the alleys
Some had eyes of steel; it felt like Death Valley

I never let one get the upper hand
If I had to throw first, I made sure it'd land

There were some scary times when they tried to take my heat
But I never got beat, was always quick on my feet

The streets can be mean; they can make a big man small
Every cop meets his match, then he turns to alcohol

So much nastiness is seen each day
Every cop takes it and buries it away

But it never really goes, sedating yourself each day
Trying to find some peace, booze, and dope to help put it away

You had a built-in filing cabinet that was shiny and new
But the drawers got rusted as the carnage grew

So you'd have to visit those alleys and parks
Like you did as a rookie when you worked in the dark

The pain never leaves, and the crime never ends
You carry those ghosts and never make amends

As you get close to the end of your career
You pray for some peace, to calmness you'll adhere

And when it all comes down to you still being on your toes
You remember what policing was like when you wore a younger man's clothes

Out On A Cliff

Now you're tired and beat up, and you're praying for the pension
   You'd be happy to trade in your gun to relieve the tension

Well, thirty years have passed, and the pension has arrived
   You're the luckiest man on earth; you finished alive

SUBPOENA DELIVERY

I was a boy detective working in a suit
Senior guys around, I started as a mute

Confidence got higher, started handling big cases
Got to know all the bad guys in town, knew all their faces

Worked around the clock, then did court all day
When you're only sleeping a few hours, it's hard to sway

One quiet Sunday, my partner said, "Suit up"
So I strapped on my gun, put on my jacket, and set down my cup

Said he had to drive north, had subpoenas to deliver
He giggled and commented, "Tonight we hurt our liver"

We drove from Brampton to Mount Forest and made one delivery
Found a local watering hole, found liquid gold like ivory

It started at the first stop, two for each double rum and Coke
Those were the days where you could have your drink and smoke

As we worked our way south, I started to see double
Stopping the unmarked on the highway to pee, I could see this would be trouble

We finally made it back to the station by twelve
Was supposed to work till three but instead put the keys on the shelf

Partner said, "Let's hit Kelsey's to finish the night off"
But we drank so much booze, we were like pigs to the trough

The best part of all, I drank all night with a gun
When I arrived at Kelsey's, they wouldn't let me have fun

I got cut off before I started for being too drunk
What irony since I just dropped off the cruiser with the shotgun in the trunk

BRAMPTON COUNTY MUNICIPAL COURT
CITY OF BRAMPTON ONTARIO   CRIMINAL TRAFFIC DIVISION
REGION OF PEEL

TIME STAMP

TO: JOHN DOE

SUBPOENA

THIS IS AN OFFICIAL NOTICE THAT THE ABOVE NAMED PARTY MUST APPEAR IN COURT AS A WITNESS.
DATE: TIME: EVENT:
JUDGE:
LOCATION:

FAILURE TO APPEAR AT THE TIME AND PLACE INDICATED MAY RESULT IN A CONTEMPT OF COURT CITATION.

HUNGOVER

A half dozen vodkas after work, liter and half of white with dinner
Barely remembered going to bed; in those days, I was a sinner

At 0315 the phone started to ring and the pager went off too
Evening shift ended at 0300 for detectives working in suits

So when the crime wave struck, day shift was called to cover 22 Division
A woman was raped, a man was arrested, the charges to be laid, my decision

My partner arrived; we formulated a plan, and I would be the notetaker
He would talk and try to get a confession, if the perp erupted, I'd be the raker

I wasn't hungover when I arrived at the station
But I was still pretty drunk, had trouble following the communication

My writing was poor and hard to read
Was feeling nauseous and needed a feed

After a while we left the room; the victim arrived from the hospital
We didn't do videos or DNA, made convictions almost impossible

Lucky for me, everyone was drunk, the victim and the bad guy
Partner said, "Not sure who smells worse, is it you or him that's high?"

We put him on ice and took a statement from the girl
Halfway through the statement, I almost had to hurl

Felt the dry heaves comin' on
Hang on, Gary, you're almost done

Now it was 0700, and the rest arrived
I couldn't believe I was still alive

Drank a ton of coffee and finally went to eat
It filled the greasy hollows; I was still on my feet

No worse feeling in the world
Working a case while your stomach's in a twirl

Out On A Cliff

Gary Rubie and Henk Rubie

DEAD ON THE FLOOR OF A BUS

Friday day shift, the last one's the best
You start days so early, really feel you need a rest

October 2, 1992
It was a sunny fall day, and the skies were blue

"22-4-10 I'm clearing you for lunch"
I'm gonna stay out; hey, dispatch, thanks a bunch

So I found a mall that the cars didn't fill
Sat alone with my coffee, be careful, don't spill

The radio was quiet that sunny afternoon
But as it is in policing, we'd be taken to the moon

"X-J-K-706, any unit to respond, no one's free for a priority one"
Dispatch, what you got? I'll cancel my lunch; you know me, volunteer for the fun

A little boy has stopped breathing on the school bus floor
The driver called it in; she's holding Mom near the door

I'm just around the corner, be there in two
I got trained in CPR; I'll know what to do

I was there in a flash; I ran straight to the bus
I can't squeeze down the aisle, but I didn't make a fuss

I lay on my stomach and pulled the boy by the hands
Now he's lying in front of me; I blew air into his glands

His body was tiny as compressions I began
He wasn't quite two, so you couldn't do it like a man

Two finger compressions on his tiny, little chest
Covered his mouth and nose with mine; no time to get stressed

More police arrived; the fire department was next
But I took full possession; I felt my muscles flex

Out On A Cliff

The ambulance was last, and when they arrived
I scooped him up and ran with the boy; I knew he would survive

Did infant CPR all the way to emerg.
When the ambulance arrived, the medical team converged

The boy was stabilized, then he went to the city
They said he was brain damaged; man, that news was shitty

They said my actions were heroic and brave
If I hadn't done CPR, he would have been in his grave

There is nothing better than saving a child's life
I went home that day, hugged my kids and my wife

Gary Rubie and Henk Rubie

OLD MAN

One thirty a.m.—911 call
Man stopped breathing, no pulse at all

I arrived with two rookies, so I controlled the scene
I knew the area well, mostly Italians is what's seen

The whole family was hysterical, deep sadness and tears
"Where's the victim?" I asked. "On the bed down the stairs"

I ran down the steps, still had my boots on
Realized it was an apartment, for the home owners' Dad and Mom

He was lying prone on the bed; I could tell he was gone
The whole family was watching, expecting me to flex my brawn

So I started CPR, with compressions on his chest
Praying the ambulance would arrive so they could do the rest

Twenty to thirty compressions and breaths into his lungs
A gurgle and then vomit shot into my mouth,
cleaned my face and the old man's tongue

Pretty sure the old guy had a massive heart attack
I couldn't do anything to save him, felt like I might yak

The rookies were stunned; they didn't know what to say
I said, "It's part of the job, you'll get it someday"

When the ambulance arrived and took the old man away
I cleared the other officers, with the family I stayed

I first used their bathroom and threw up myself
Then we sat and had tea, trying to put the tragedy on the shelf

The family was grateful for the efforts I made
For taking the time to explain and for coming to their aid

About a month later, a letter came to the chief
Commending my actions for helping them through their grief

Out On A Cliff

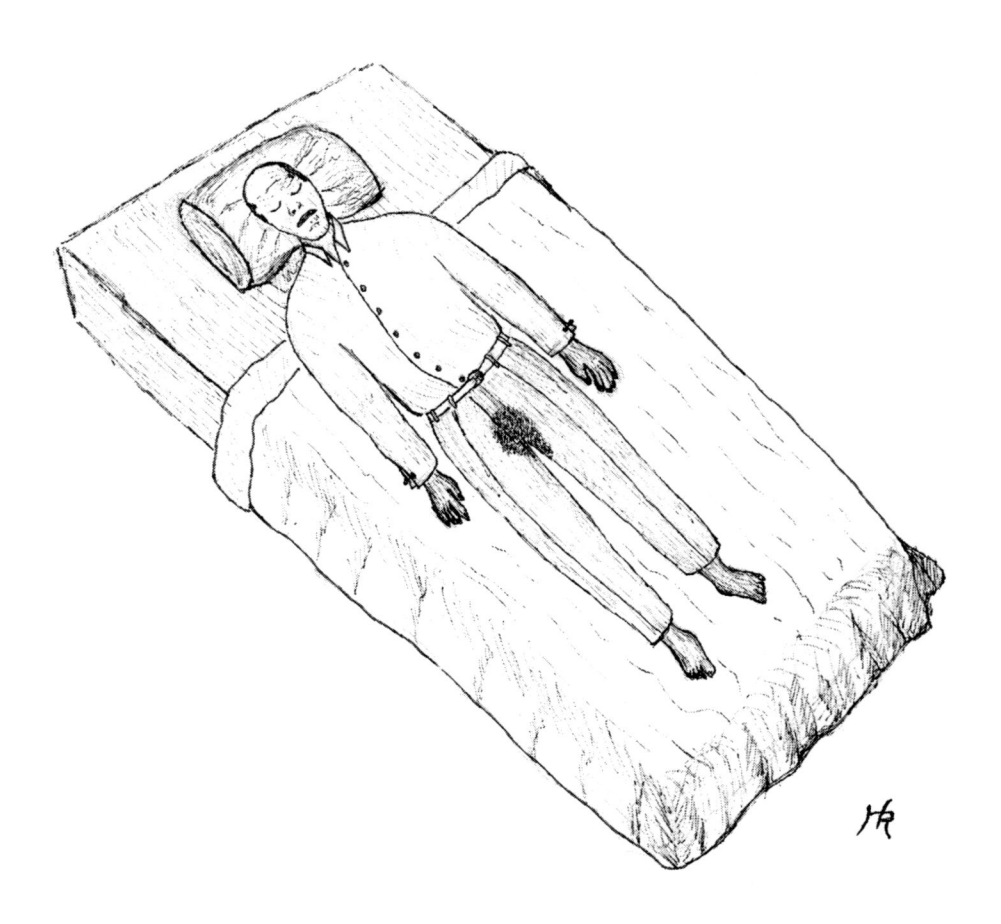

Gary Rubie and Henk Rubie

THE TAXI

Another call for service, middle of the day
Drunk in a taxi may have passed away

Arrived before the ambulance, always seems the way
7-Eleven parking lot would be the end of this guy's day

Noticed a man in his forties slumped in the backseat
He had soiled himself; on the floor was vomit and false teeth

I ain't going near this one, I said in my head
The smell in the back of the taxi I was beginning to dread

A crowd had gathered, other officers arrived
I suggested they climb in the taxi to see if he's alive

They said, "You were here first, this is your call"
If the crowd hadn't gathered, I would have cursed them all

"Somebody do something!" a bystander yelled
So I crawled in on top of that god-awful smell

My memory went back to the old man who puked in my mouth
At that very moment, I wished I was on a plane going south

So I covered his mouth and pretended to blow
A couple of compressions, to him that much I owed

Every good cop knows when the bile and bowels go
There's no saving the victim; you just put on a show

The ambulance arrived and saw the state he was in
They whispered, "He's dead." Do we know next of kin?

They put him on a stretcher, put his teeth in a bag
Drove away to the hospital, displaying the black flag

I got in my cruiser to follow them there
Get the smell from my nostrils, breathe deep the fresh air

OUT ON A CLIFF

HOW CLOSE YOU CAME

He followed you into the bathroom stall,
Two grown men gonna play eight ball

I went in first, then my partner followed,
I booted the door, then you flushed and swallowed

I saved the goods and held on tight,
Dragged you out and stood you upright

Anything in here, anything in there,
No, sir, nothing that I'd like to share

Keep your hands on the wall, don't make no fist,
Hang on a minute, copper, you want some of this?

And without hesitation, he raised up one hand,
Holding shining silver, sending me to the promised land

Push hard, draw down, pull the trigger, step away,
But my instincts were not going to fail me on this day

I grabbed the steel with both free hands,
Striking elbows and knees wherever they'd land

Got control of the steel, went into a blind haze,
Blood was everywhere; partner was dazed

He came so close on that fateful night,
A .38 between the eyes could have been his plight

And in the end when complaints were made,
The color of his skin turned a little jade

Out On A Cliff

Suck it up, you piece of shit
You were the one who tried the hit

You failed at life, you lost the game,
I would be embarrassed to use your name

'Cause in the end, during the curtain call,
Your entire life was one big fall

THE PLAY

Walked in alone; the game had begun
All the good sense about me said "Get up and run"

Entered into a darkness where no man should go
Money lined my pockets, a head full of blow

Keep breathing deeply; try not to sweat
Stay super cool; it's not over yet

Throw the line into the water; be sure the bait is snug
Don't go with the dancer; don't let her give you a hug

Keep the chess game going; stay two moves ahead
Don't let your guard down, or you'll end up dead

Pull gently on the line; start to reel the bait in
Don't get to high; got a belly full of gin

Now you've closed the house deal, time to hand over their keys
One wrong move, and everyone is going down to their knees

The deed has been signed; the house has been sold
Once again you came out alive, looking like gold

How many years did this one take, what's gonna be the toll?
Keep on living like a fake; one fine day, my head will roll

Even balls the size of church bells one day will end up small
Living out there on the edge of the cliff, looking down the face of the wall

So I look back on my time—were they years that were well spent?
I lost a nickel here, a dime there, but my mind is forever bent

So it's filed into the dark place, a space far within my head
Not to be revisited—staying with me until I'm dead

OUT ON A CLIFF

103

THE CALLBACK

Had dinner with the family, then burned a big fatty
Felt like eating another meal and got a little chatty

Stanley Cup Finals on the tube, just settled in
Was going to triple overtime; Hull would score and win

Then the phone went off; boss said it was time to roll
Why's it always so late with these damn assholes?

The electronic device we planted, GPS in his car
Had him eastbound on the 401, but just how far?

When we finally stopped, the computer showed we're in a suburb of Montreal
Grabbed a quick shut-eye because soon he was going to fall

He was in for six hours; we liaised with the Montreal cops
When our boy started west, he took a bag, made no stops

Montreal did a warrant on the house that we sat and watched
Had four "kilos" of blow that our guy left there when he stopped

We did a high-risk takedown on the 401 going west
Seized a suitcase full of cash; everyone was stressed

By then it was late Sunday morning, and my kids were up
They made gifts for me, Father's Day, but Dad was gone, he was a cop . . .

You can never retrieve those lost precious moments
The kids don't understand; Dad's not there for presents

Well, you'd worked around the clock, and you were finally home
You found everyone sleeping, nasty note, you were all alone

Working undercover takes years from your life
After all my years, I lost more than most—my kids and my wife

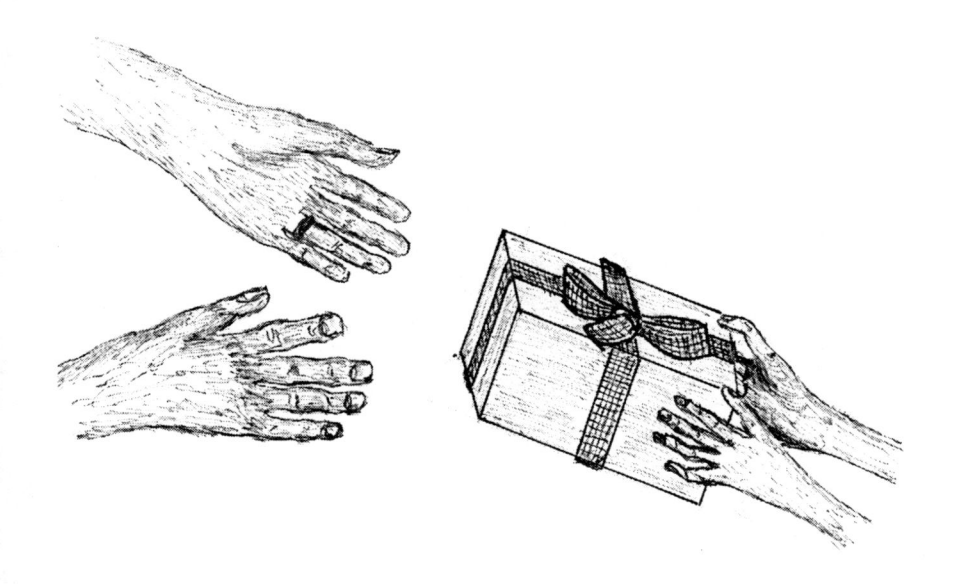

BROKEN

Broken hearts and broken dreams
Life's just never what it seems

Sliding down a slippery slope
Full of fear, have no hope

Sometimes wishing time to stand still
Can't I just take a magic pill?

Push so hard to make ends meet
Some days I can barely stand on my feet

What's going on? I want it to stop
Why the hell did I become a cop?

You spend your career dealing with strife
Take the pain to your grave, carry it for life

Lived the life of ten grown men
It was like thirty years spent in the pen

Hatred, Anger, Fury, and Rage
Someone let me out of this cage

They sit in their leather on the mountaintop
Judging the men about being a cop

Thinking they're so smart, didn't miss a beat
None of them remember what it's like on the street

So judge all you want; I don't answer to you
My maker will judge me when my day is through

Out On A Cliff

YOUR REIGN OF TERROR

You thought you walked the righteous line
You shattered moral while serving your time

Broke the spirit of good men and women
Your reign of terror is to be proven

You protected yourself, gave your friends the power
When it's all said and done, this won't be your hour

You continue to keep the blue bloodline flowing
But when we cut your veins, we'll stop corruption from growing

So line up your lawyers and all your henchmen
'Cuz when we are done, you rats are in the pen

For three brothers from the valley have taken a stand
To fight the machine and the corrupt boss man

When they rally the troops and gain their support
Each one of these pricks will end up in court

Then judgment day will be seen by all
And the dirty bloodline will finally fall

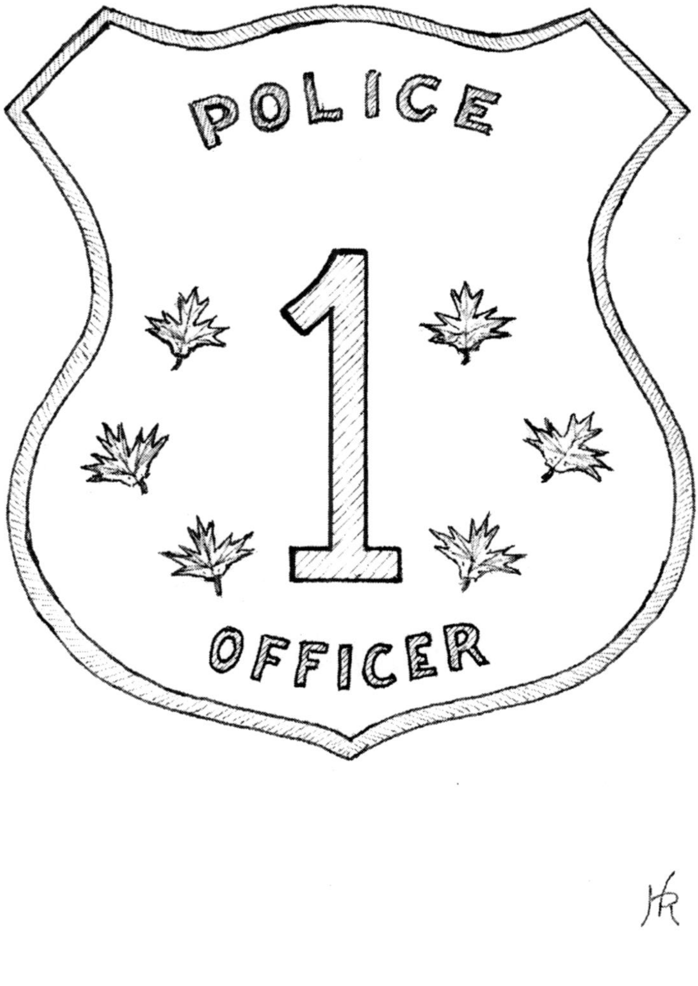
POLICE
1
OFFICER

THE STRUCTURE

The base of the pyramid supports the peak
But the man at the top is just a big geek

Surrounds himself with bullies and power
Lives his life from hour to hour

These men of power erode the foundation
But remain untouched due to insulation

The real strength and power is down on the street
But the man and his machine won't protect the beat

As the spokes in the wheel continue to break
The man and his henchmen forget what's at stake

So when it all crumbles and the pyramid comes down
The geek at the top will be forced to the ground

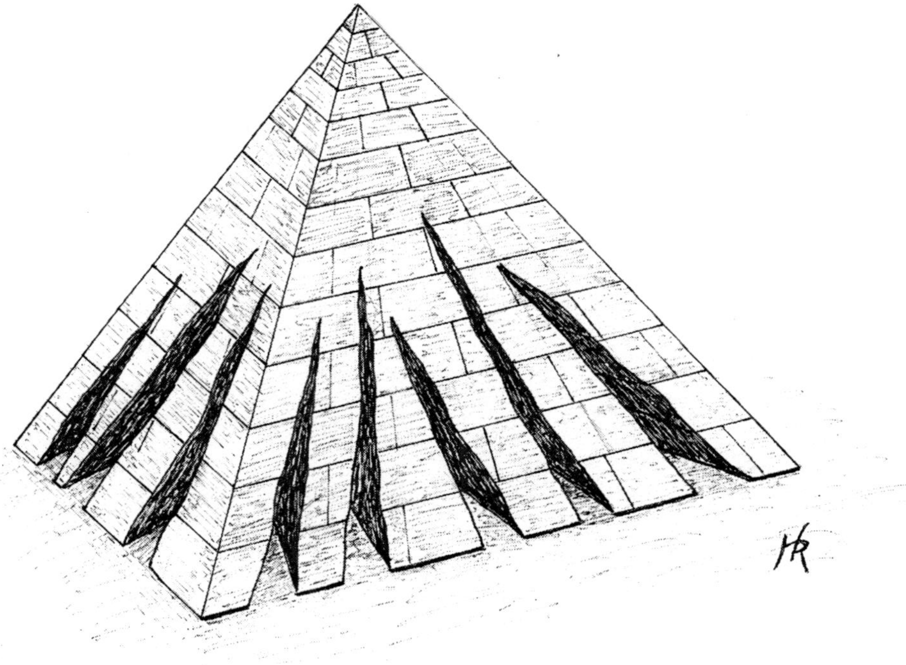

ALL TAKE AND NO GIVE

I gave and I gave, and you took and you took
One-way streets are for users and crooks

The lights turn on when the skies get dark
The takers keep taking like a walk in the park

They stroll hand in hand 'cuz there's power in numbers
Run a knife through their wrists, and they suddenly flounder

Hardball's the only game that they know
Sneak up behind them, keep quiet, be slow

When you're close enough to strike the first shot
Strike quick, strike often, keep strikin' a lot

Be completely relentless and don't ever give in
Until that knockout blow lands square on the chin

When you catch the sweet spot and they do the face-plant
Keep filling 'em up, squish 'em hard like an ant

Don't feel any shame, and screw all the guilt
Now it's your turn to take; the tables will tilt

Out On A Cliff

CHILD PORN

I was the first cop on Peel to go online
Pretending I was twelve was not a crime

Was the first cop in Canada to run a covert course
Had an expert from Chicago share his knowledge, a good source

Spent many hours in predicated sites
They pounce like sharks on fresh bloody bites

They steal little boys and snatch little girls
They promise them gifts and love and pearls

They caused terrible damage to the body and the mind
Hiding inside the computer makes them hard to find

And when we'd catch one, the job got hard
We'd review their whole collection of children scarred

Hundreds of thousands of disturbing cries
Videos full of pain I watched in their young eyes

Never ever in my twenty-five years
Did I experience such pain, it brought me to tears

What really caused me heartache and pain
Was the judicial system and the sentencing that came

They say that your kind is mentally sick
But my cure for you is to cut off your dick

Out On A Cliff

NUMB

Did I just see what I think I saw? Was what I saw real?
Has mankind become so dysfunctional? Why doesn't my body feel?

The more disturbing things I get exposed to as a cop
The more numb I feel, and it just won't stop

So back in '84, I wanted to try to feel
I sat in the chair for my very first tattoo and felt a pain that was real

It seemed that every shift, I drove the car with a cage
Was like driving a dump truck from call to call until I felt the rage

So I'd wait 'til days off, then go and see my friend Rick
I sat in the chair, and he carved me up, getting inked did the trick

It would hold me over a month, a year, until the next time I got numb
Often I would revisit the chair, sometimes with a belly full of rum

And each time I left, I felt a little sting
It just gave me something to hang on to and cling

Twenty-four times I've sat in that chair
But I stopped feeling pain, so I turned to prayer

When prayer didn't work, I turned to what I knew best
Got my hands on booze and dope and put it in my chest

That was a terrible spiral I put everyone through
Several times I thought for sure my life was through

I crawled out of that garbage can and learned a simpler life
I didn't have to fall on the sword or die by the edge of a knife

Out On A Cliff

THE JUNTAS

I served your region and the citizens within
I did your thick dirty so you remained insulated and thin

I played the game hurt for twenty-five years
You condemned me for coping with a few dozen beers

And when my pain got too great and I started to fall
You turned your back on me and didn't help me at all

You began to fight me every step of the way
You forgot how I took care of you back in the day

But I ain't a rat; that's not what this is about
You punked as you climbed your arrogant ladder of clout

I won't tell tales about the dirt under your nails
I won't share your dirty stories, won't give out details

But one thing's for sure, and I'll share with you now
I'm done being your doormat; you can't make me bend over and bow

I won't play on your team, won't do your dirt anymore
You can have your *jersey* back; I lost pride in what I wore

The flash was stitched on my shoulder and etched into my heart
Today nothing makes me happier than that the flash and I did part

Out On A Cliff

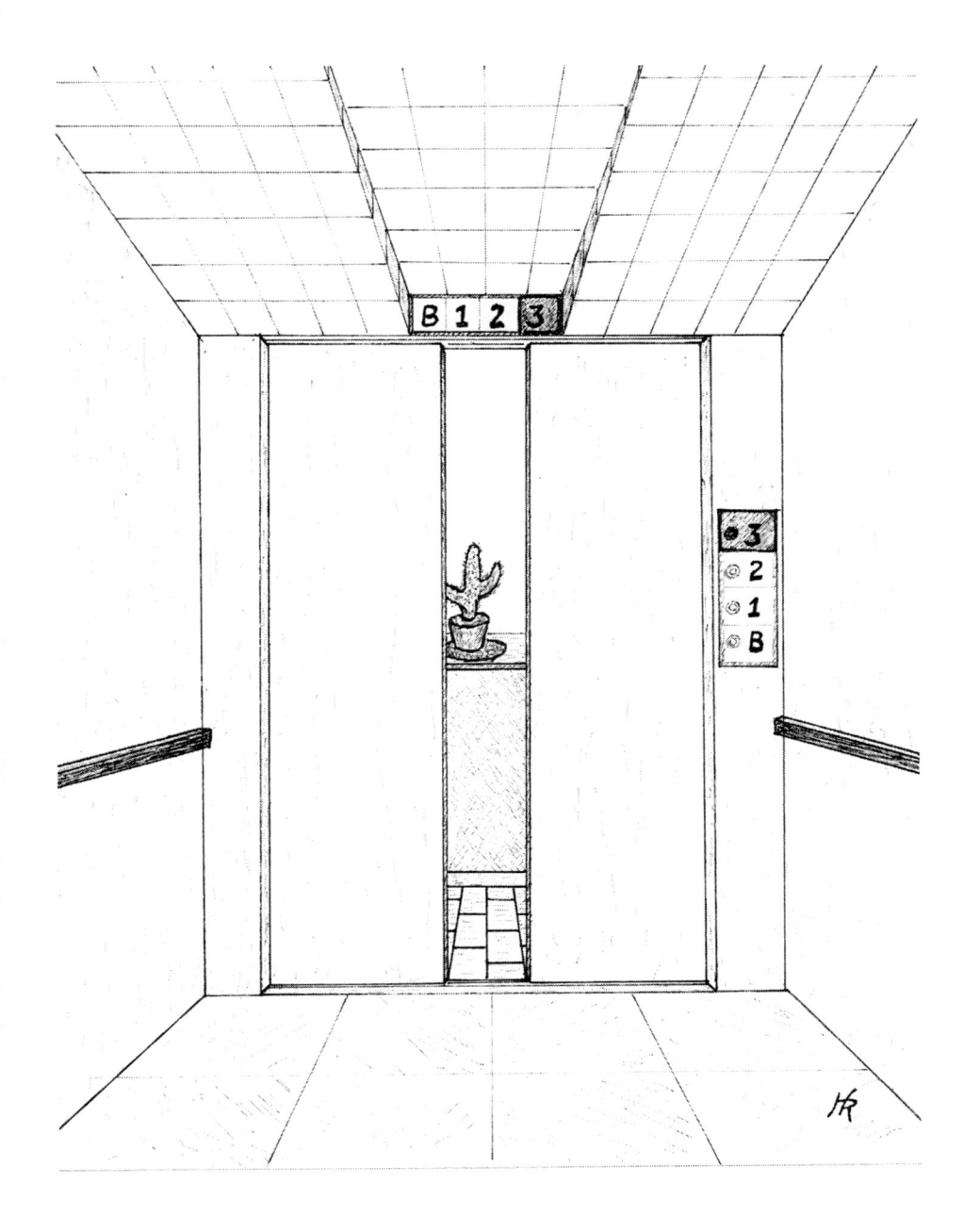

RATS WITH HATS

I worked for two female rats at two different times
Intimidated them both with my experience, which they could not find

The female detectives who shared one brain
Tried to do a sewer's job and frame my name

My reputation they trashed was more importantly on the line
But this copper can cover his ass, as others tried to fuck with his mind

So the two-headed split ass with only one brain
Were pissed 'cuz I was smarter and wouldn't play their game

Twenty-one years of excellent evaluations, but then they lied
I would show them who was smarter and defend my name with pride

They typed up pure bullshit and handed it off to Glenn
His spineless handoff wouldn't get the signature of my pen

So I reviewed my file, copied every evaluation
Typed a five-page rebuttal; it destroyed their damnation

I scared the head cheese; he asked, "Were there more copies?"
He would fix it himself and then tell the rats they were sloppies

I wasn't stupid; I knew the cover-up plan
Kept copies of everything, human rights complaint in hand

And so it goes, ranking officers bullying subordinates
None of them ever scared me; I couldn't give two shits

Best part of all, the head cheese said he'd make it right
But he didn't have the balls to get my back and fight

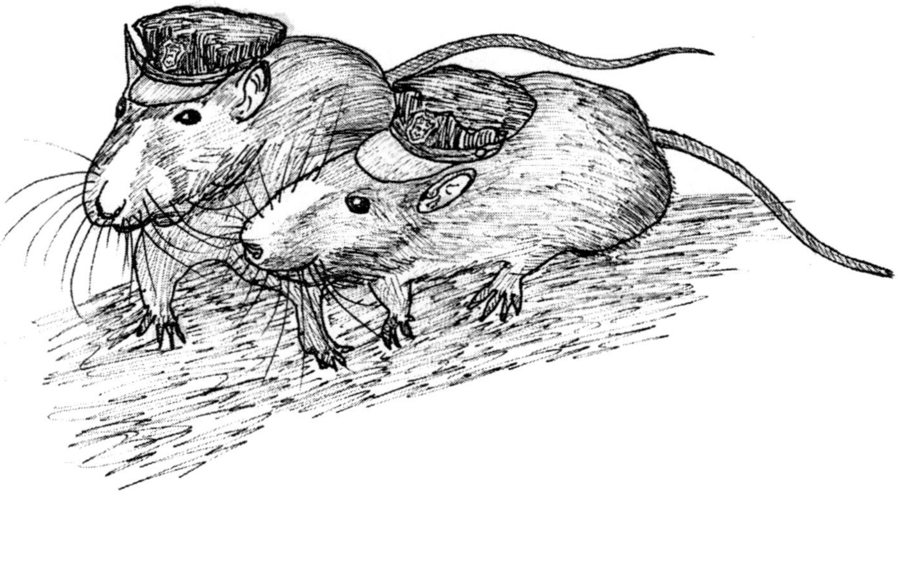

NO REGRETS

No regrets for where I've been
No regrets for what I've seen

No regrets for whom I hurt
My scars are covered by my shirt

No regrets for all my loss
I realize now, I'm not the boss

No regrets for how hard I played
For crying for help, I begged——I prayed

No regrets for the broken marriage
I never promised a white horse and carriage

No regrets for all my crime
Was so damn lucky I didn't do time

My time was serving the streets of Peel
It ripped out my heart; I forgot how to feel

Today I live a pure, clean life
Maybe someday, I'll take a new wife

I'll have no regrets when my time is done
I'll live clean every day, with each rising sun

NO REGRETS

MY CAREER (1133)

The journey has taken you to many dark places
Met some good people, always seeing new faces

Twenty-five years have just flown by
Take a deep breath, look up to the sky

You got nothing to prove, been there, done that
You've swallowed the sword; you've worn the hat

So you cruise by yourself into the last five
Working like a bee, creating your hive

And when three decades have come to a close
You'll come out the other side smelling like a rose

You'll have a gold watch and a championship ring
But the watch and ring really won't mean a thing

'Cuz in the end, the pension's where it's at
You lived nine lives, like an alleyway cat

But the truth be told, you survived at least ten
You know you're going to heaven; you just don't know when

"1133"

Gary Rubie and Henk Rubie

UNTOUCHABLE EGO

Sitting in a satin chair
Handful of gel in my hair

Decked out in my Sunday best
In my head, I'm better than the rest

No one can touch me; I wear a giant cape
On the cape is a big S to help me escape

Bullets, knives, fast-driving cars
I can dodge them all; I can fly to Mars

You see, I was superhuman and controlled the world
Seven feet ten, I'd cut you and watch your blood swirl

You didn't penetrate my sheet of armor
One minute I was a badass, the next I was a charmer

The arrogance I carried was thick and foul
You could smell my bullshit like a buffalo's bowel

It's probably what kept me alive in those days
Worked undercover, bought dope in a dive, under a soft purple haze

The intensity was always so high, so much was at stake
But I craved the chaos; to do the next buy, I couldn't wait

Then one day it all came crashing down
I lost the juice, felt mortal, felt down

I had to make a move, and it had to be soon—ask God
So I traded in my hash pipe for a pocket protector in fraud

Little did I know that the druggies I dealt with
Were now committing fraud to help get them stiff

Eventually I left it all behind for a better life
Something safe and lucrative for the kids and the wife

Out On A Cliff

Then the towers came down, and I went running back
I made a mistake leaving, even if it meant risking a heart attack

Nine more years have passed, and I've paid the ultimate price
I broke in half like a branch in a storm; PTSD isn't nice

MY PAIN

Oh, how I wish that the pain would stop
It tortures my mind from bottom to top

My soul screams and cries, like a child on a breast
Can't make it slow down, can't make it rest

There must be an end to all this madness
I don't have the answer; I just want gladness

I feel like I'm dying a little each day
It just has to get better, or I may not stay

Everyone says that time heals all
But after each step forward comes a backward fall

Starting to feel like I'm running in quicksand
Why can't I find the answers while I'm on this land?

A wise friend told me, "Practice patience and faith"
But time's slipping away, my weekdays need an eighth

I have to stay positive and believe there's a fix
Suicide's not an option; I won't be carried by six

I got too much to offer, much left to do
This depression will pass; I'll stop feeling blue

I'm on the verge of greatness, about to start a new life
I lived by the sword, and I died by the knife

The job took its toll, cut me into little pieces
But I've ironed out the wrinkles, flattened out the creases

I'll take my early pension, won't sell myself short
The last twenty-five years was like playing a professional sport

Need to rest the body, then heal the mind
Played through the injuries, through every grind

Out On A Cliff

So just for today, maybe just for the hour
I'll make myself smile and look like a flower

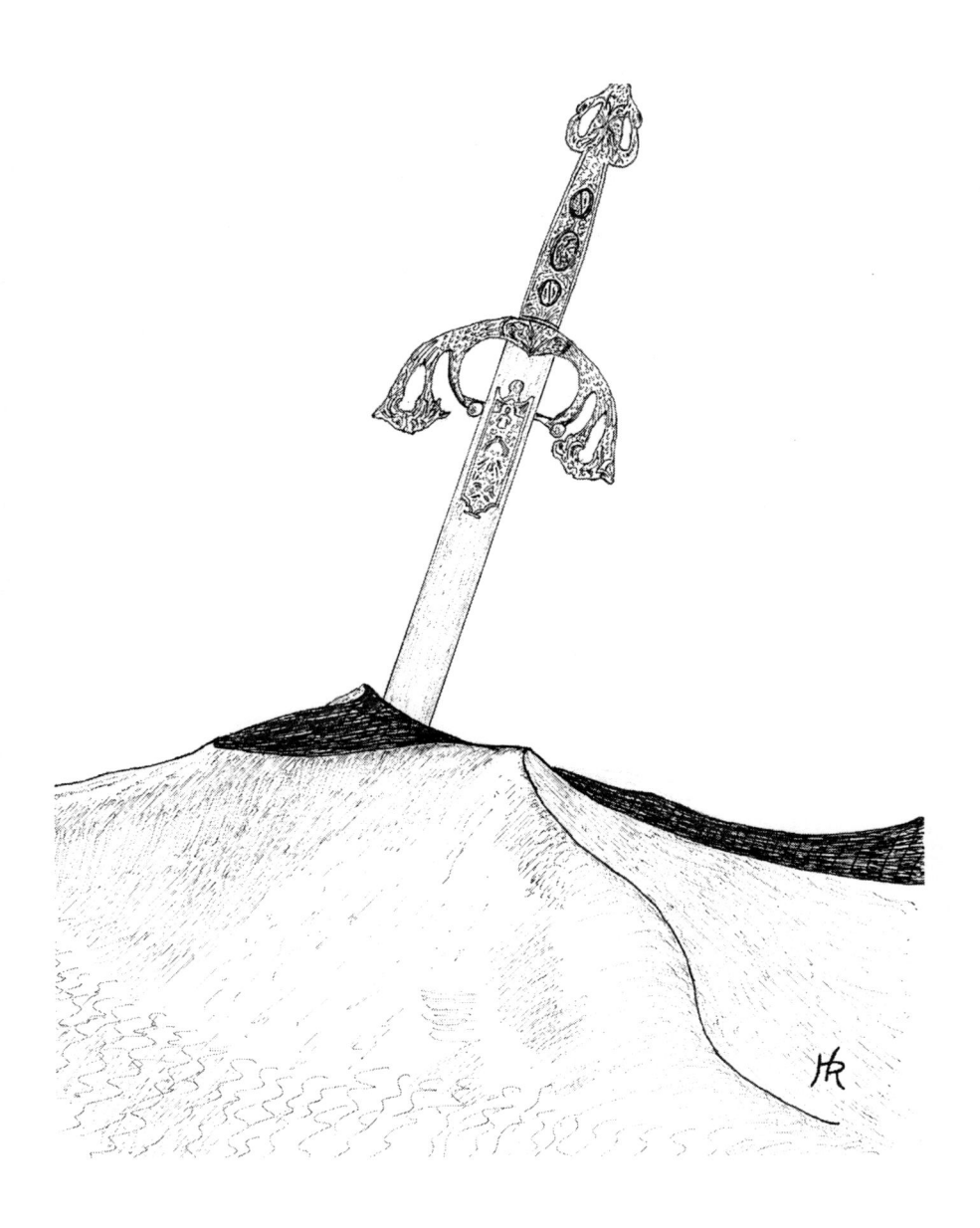

PTSD

The fear starts to mount as the day draws near
What will the answer be? What will I hear?

I've given twenty-five long, painful years of my life
I've battled the whole journey through happiness and strife

My wings have been earned many times over
I'm lucky to be alive, had my four-leaf clover

But now I sit and suffer all alone
Became so tired, just wanna go home

However home isn't where this train ride's gone
Something terrible has happened; it's all become wrong

PTSD is the heavy price I paid
Feeling so down, knew I shouldn't have stayed

I had a chance to run back in 2001
But I didn't get far, came back for more fun

But the treadmill didn't stop, couldn't slow my brain down
I should have kept running right out of town

So here I am, alone, doing time
Can't call out for help, can't drop a dime

They medicate my mind, tell me get lots of rest
The pills make me mellow; I think it's all just a test

Now the time has arrived, and soon I will know
If they make me return to where I don't want to go

I met with incompetence, but I got a lift
Her lack of knowledge became a gift

No need to hide or enter back doors
Going through the front, I'll get much more

The answer lies in telling the truth
The reports from the doctors will be the proof

ADDICTIONS

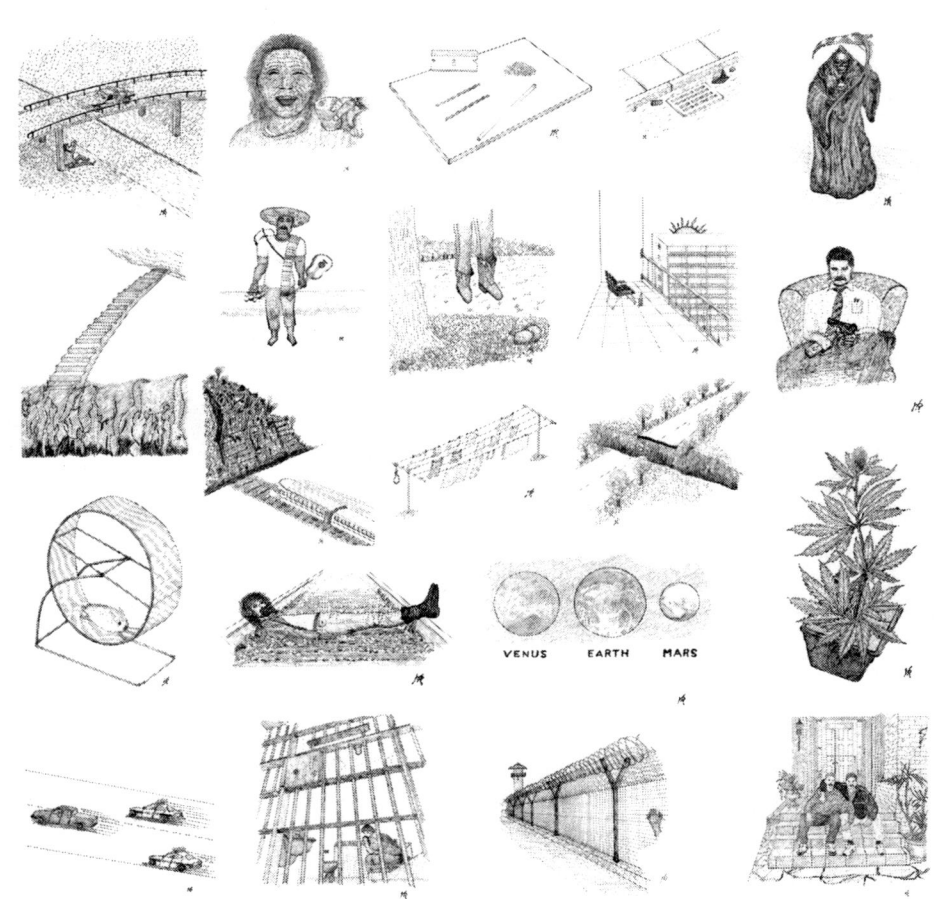

ROUND AND ROUND

Round and round and round we go
Where it lets us off, who the hell knows?
Takes us to the bitter end
Chews us up, then we start over again

Round and round and round we go
One day's high and one day's low
Each day you walk down a different street
Wearing someone else's feet

Round and round and round we go
Feeling like an average joe
Can't think clear, can't think straight
The life that I began to hate

Round and round and round I swing
Trying to find a better thing
The game of life ain't always so kind
Sometimes messing up your mind

Round and round and round I fall
Sometimes big and sometimes small
And so for today I stopped going around
Keeping my feet planted on the ground

OUT ON A CLIFF

THE MORNING DRINK
THE EVENING HANGOVER

Back in the day, I worked in uniform patrol
The demon alcohol had already taken control

Worked a three-shift rotation, which included nights
Every five weeks, went in for seven and fights

And every morning I'd get home at eight
Craved through the night for the drink I couldn't wait

That's when the morning cocktail first caught my taste
Coming home in the morning and straight to bed seemed such a waste

In those early days, lived on the fifteenth floor
Drank my beers or some whiskeys, whatever I could pour

The sunrise cocktail always seemed to do the trick
Helped bury the horrors of swinging the nightstick

Having just enough booze would make night terrors disappear
But I would wake up hungover at night, craving beers

Starting work at midnight hungover and groggy
Chasing devils under the stars is dangerous when you're foggy

When 8:00 a.m. arrived and I survived another shift
I'd hit my balcony with my bottle till my mind was adrift

Out On A Cliff

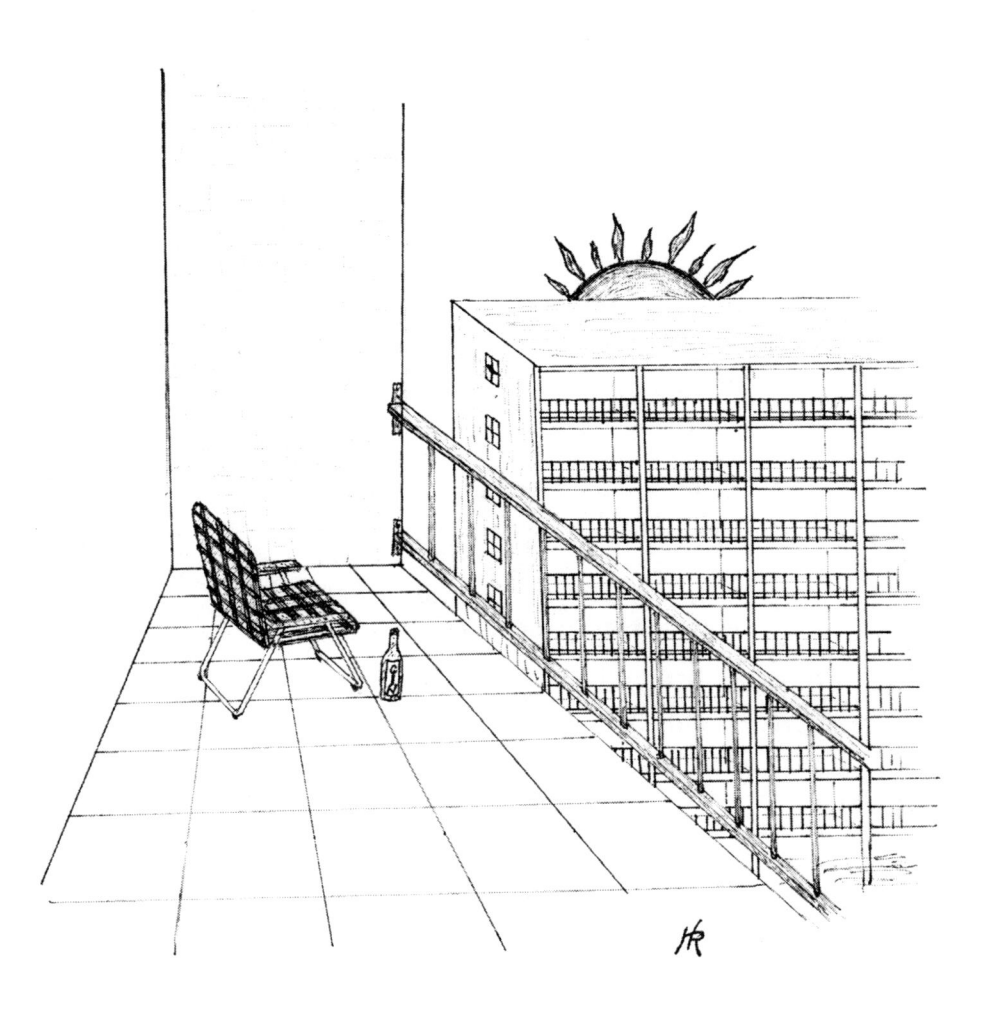

BRIGS AND BENNY

Brownie and Blackie couldn't be pulled apart
Two longtime amigos that made drinking an art

Their history is rich and storied with thrills
They drank an ocean of whiskey, ate a mountain of pills

One was a PI, the other was a cop
No matter what they did, you couldn't get them to stop

Always had each other's back, never ratted each other out
Played real hard . . . ran with the devil . . . professions carried clout

There were many great road trips in the Econoline van
Through all four seasons, they drank, smoked, and ran

One real good time was "A-bomb" on the Grand
Brownie always captured the moment with a Nikon in hand

The insanity level got high from *Barfly* to *Where the Buffalo Roam*
Never afraid to give everything a try, and most nights didn't come home

One crazy-ass night, super stoked in Nic's Tavern
Brownie picked the corner pocket to relieve in a cavern

They were the only two playin' eight ball in the bar
Brownie wanted to snatch from the till and bolt for the car

They were lucky he didn't; for sure they'd do time
Snatching money is robbery, and that's a real crime

They survived all those years; they were crazy but fun
They did nutty shit and even once used a gun

They both got married, and then kids came along
For a little bit longer, they played the same song

That was so long ago; they slowed their lives down
But I'll always remember when Blackie and Brownie ran the town

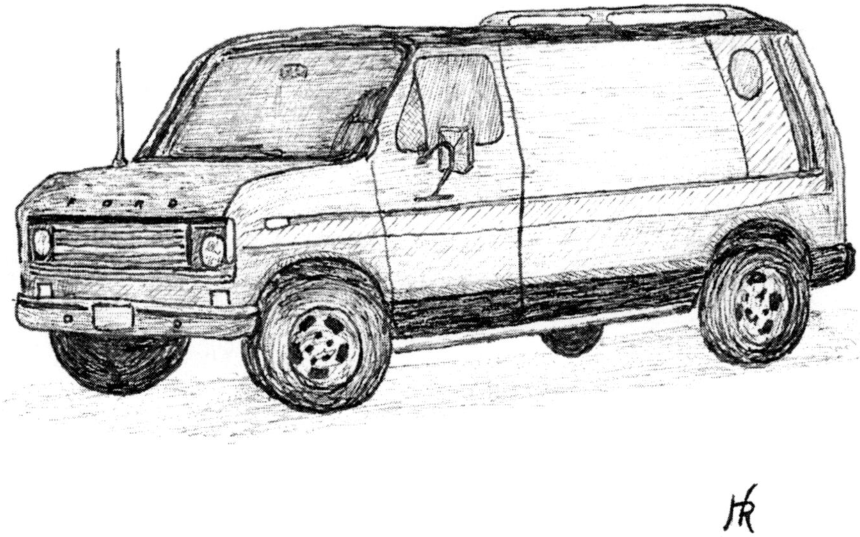
FORD

CLOSET

Locked in a closet, couldn't get out
Screamed all night; no one heard my shout

Locked in a closet, give me the key
Who's got the combination, is it you or me?

Locked in a closet, clawing on the walls
Do you hear the footsteps running down the halls?

Locked in a closet, starting to shake, starting to sweat
Was that an earthquake? This nightmare over yet?

Locked in a closet, now I've loaded the gun
Do I face my demons, or do I turn and run?

Locked in a closet, I hear the voices again
I can't stand the insanity; let me out of this pen

Locked in a closet, put the barrel in my mouth
If I pull the trigger now, I'll end up in the south

Locked in a closet, don't surrender to the pain
Swing the door open; learn to live life again

Locked in a closet . . .

BARSTOOL

Sitting on a barstool, always bellied up
Come on, my new friend, fill up my cup

Keep the booze flowing; don't ever stop
Not leavin' this chair till I finish every drop

Line up the squadron, then tequila for all
Flying the B-52, I know I won't fall

Another shot of courage; I'm not there quite yet
Where are my kids? Who's watching my pet?

My vision is blurry; one more for the ditch
Any brooms in the back to take home to my witch?

Now that I'm primed, propped up on my stool
Acting real crazy, I look like a fool

Call me a cab; I just can't drive home
Looks like I'm sleeping on the couch, all alone

Won't do this tomorrow; I can't find my car
But once the sun rises, I'm right back at the bar

Out On A Cliff

THE DARKNESS

You led me to the darkness
What were you trying to teach?
Climbing up the face of a mountain
Was I that far outta reach?

You led me to the darkness
The journey was slow and cold
The pain that I was feeling
Began to make me feel real old

You led me to the darkness
A path that was full of pain
A fork in the road, so I took it again
Thoughts swelling within my brain

You took me to the darkness
Full of hate, anger, and resentment
Tired, alone, and restless
Unable to locate the contentment

You took me to the darkness
I began to see the way
Hope was placed before me
Darkness replaced by the light of day

OUT ON A CLIFF

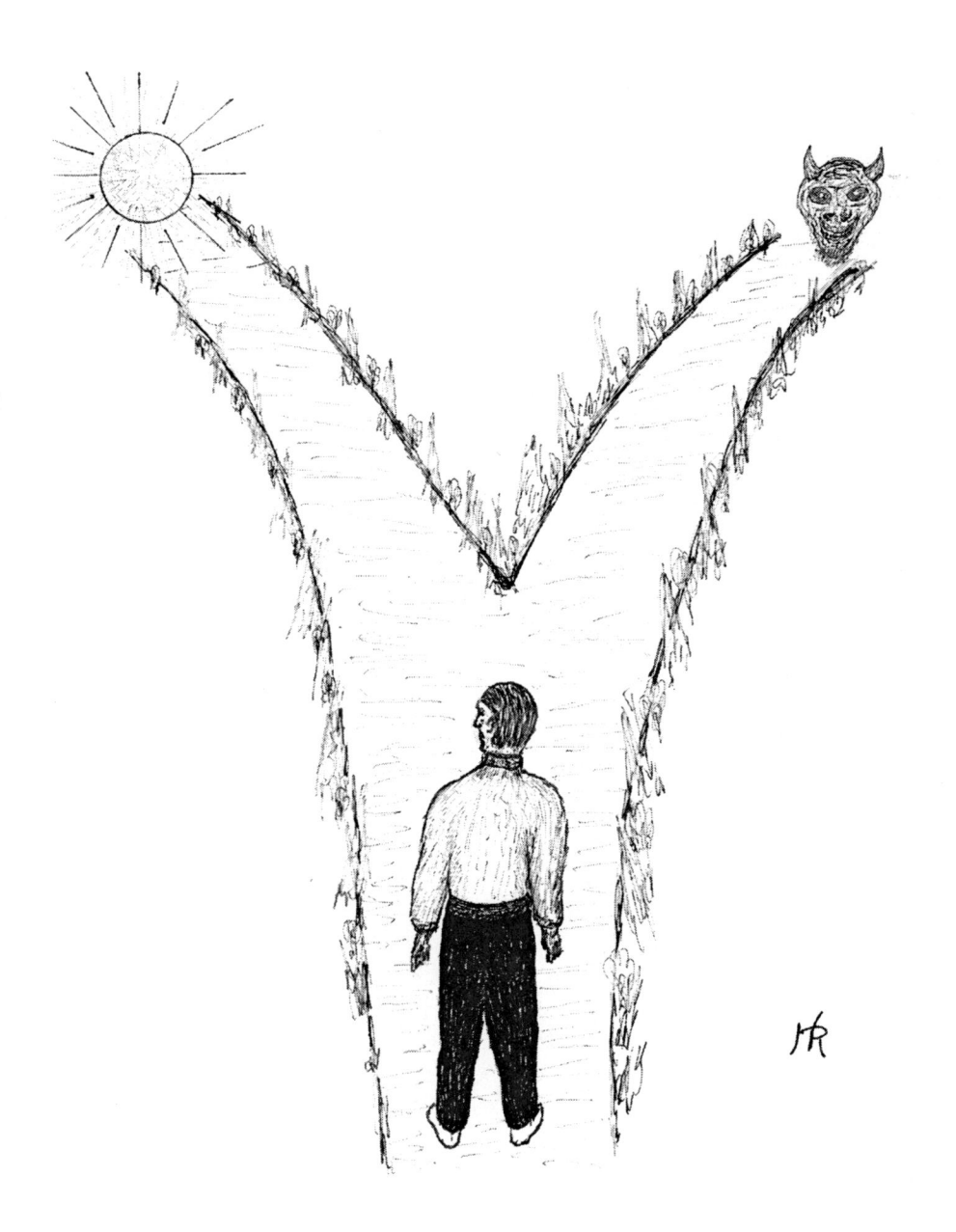

STAIRCASE TO HELL

The holes get deeper as I stumble and fall
I was attacked from behind by the cunning and baffling alcohol

A power so great, felt I had no control
I was spinning so bad, saw myself as a bridge troll

Shame and sadness, fear and emotionally bankrupt
I hated the image staring back from the cup

It's been three to four months since I last spoke to God
I need his help now, maybe sharpen the rod

Take a deep breath, put routine back in my day
Bring back God; he can help so I don't sway

Having structure and routine will keep me outta my head
There aren't many holes left; next time I may be dead

I can't seem to find my stairway to heaven
But many times I've fallen down the staircase to hell

I've been told by the recovered to practice being grateful
When you're knocked down seven times, make sure you get up eight

My rage continues to grow, and I feel I'm full of hate
I'm trying to find a happy place, a place that won't lock the gate

I can't afford to hold anger and rage, that luxury I don't possess
For if I do keep it buried deep, my life will be a mess

I can't allow myself to fall down the staircase of hell
I know I've gotta take a different stairway in order to feel well

Out On A Cliff

RELAPSE

Got off the plane, fell flat on my face
I'm such an embarrassment; what a disgrace

I came to have fun, to bring us together
What I gave them instead was insecurity and stormy weather

I instilled lots of fear, made them wish they were home
Couldn't stay away from the devil; I really should be alone

But the problem with me is, when I'm by myself
I don't have any feelings, like my life's on a shelf

Get it together; pull my shit tight and straight
If I keep screwing up, I'll end up in a crate

So once and for all, live one day at a time
And get to a phone; put in the dime

Ask for help; get off my high horse
I can only get better; it can't get worse

Thank God I'm alive; I lived through the hell
Keep it together, and I just might get well

Out On A Cliff

REFLECTION

I looked in the mirror and saw myself staring back
The closer I looked, the more the mirror cracked

The broken image staring back at me
Was a picture of what I used to be

Memories and dreams that have long since left
Like a precious piece of art taken in a theft

I tried to make sense of what I'd become
Pretended to be a winner but really felt like a bum

For the face that I saw staring back was not fake
But the reality of my world made it hard for me to take

And often I thought what it would be like to leave
But the vision of my kids crying made my stomach heave

So I put those thoughts to the back of my head
Even though I felt I'd be better off dead

But death wasn't where my life was to go
Have to learn to live clean with my kids in tow

'Cuz I know that somewhere my soul mate lies waiting
So I live with patience, searching and dating

But I won't push too hard 'cuz I do believe in fate
And for that very reason, I have to sit back and wait

Wait for that woman to come into my life
And remove me from this insane world of strife

So my kids grow older, and I become humble
I try to walk straight, upright, and not stumble

Out On A Cliff

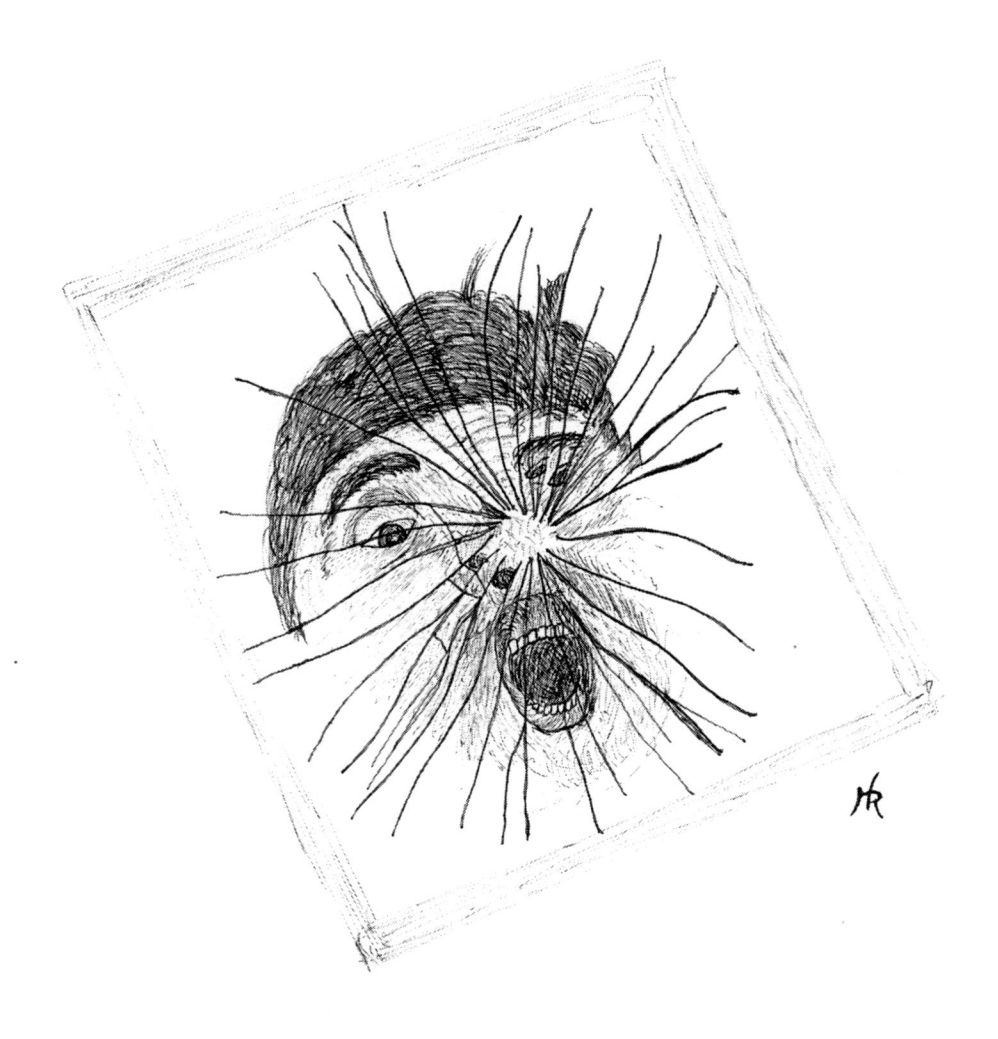

INSANITY DEFINED

You led me to edge of the cliff; my fear of heights was gone
I couldn't see the ground below, but the drop wouldn't take me long

The fall would be quick; the pain would be great
A horrible hurt for which I couldn't wait

Start right away; don't turn back now
'Cuz you know when it's done, they'll just ask how

How did the switch turn on yet again?
Who opened the door, why'd you open the pen?

Did you think the result wouldn't be the same?
But it only showed the world that you really are insane

Repeating the same actions, expecting different results
Makes everyone around you do somersaults

Like laundry in the dryer, if it spins long enough
It won't just dry out; it get's leathery and tough

So unplug the machine, hang the clothes on the line
Let the wind blow them dry, then they'll all be just fine

Out On A Cliff

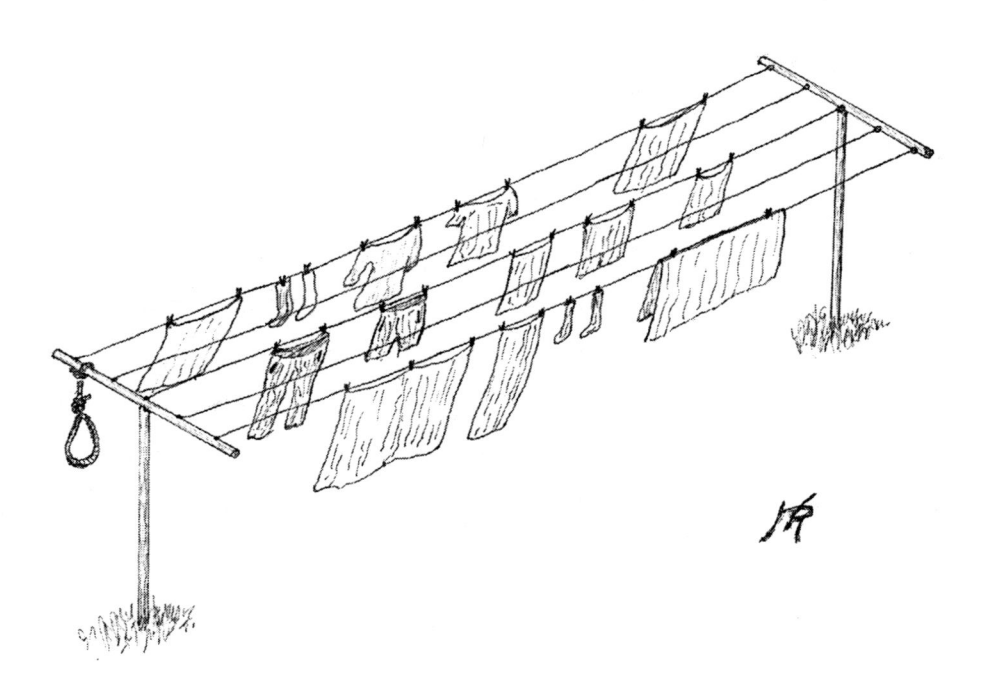

WATER UNDER THE BRIDGE

The alarm went off at 4:35; had Sunday day shift ahead
Still drunk from the bender on Saturday night, I felt like I was dead

Called the boss man, can't make it in today
Got a touch of food poisoning just the other day

Went back to bed and missed the 0600 shift, woke up around 1100
Still felt sick and I was coming around, but this surely wasn't heaven

The lady I was with took away my keys; she said, "I won't let you drive"
Tried to block my way from leaving the house; I told her, "Don't even try"

So off I went into the blizzard that turned to freezing rain
First stop was the Longo's—they had a wine cellar; I need to kill my pain

A cheap bottle of sherry at 18 percent just might do the trick
Where can I drink it? I'm in the middle of town, maybe I'll go to the crick

Slid down the snow and under the bridge, protected from the freezing rain
Took off the cap and threw it away, took a guzzle for my brain

Suddenly a man appeared, chain-smoking darts without words
I thought I was crazy, but this dude creeped me out;
his behavior seemed so absurd

The bottle was two-thirds gone, and I thought it was time to go
So I approached the silent chain-smoking man and handed my bottle slow

He didn't say thanks, just took my offering, and guzzled the rest of it down
I walked away and started to climb the slippery slope like a clown

As I made the crest on my hands and knees, reaching for the rails
I felt a shame beyond anything before, and what I saw made me pale

Driving across the bridge was one of my guys in a fully marked cruiser
And there I was climbing, trying to hide my face; I felt like such a loser

Out On A Cliff

Ended up in two bars, then made it home; friend said, "Trying to phone yah"
I hit the bed, and when I awoke, I had the walking pneumonia

Another lesson learned, another bottom hit on the train of self-destruction
Please let me off at the very next stop; my recovery is under construction

REAPER TAKER

The reaper paid a call just the other day
Brought a bag of goodies to make a big man sway

Dropped the buffalo to his knees, made him beg for his life
I'll crank it up if you please, don't let go, don't hang on to tight

He was once my dear friend, came looking for my soul
Battled against him all these years, began to take its toll

I struggled and I fought to gain self-respect
Amazed I ain't been caught; oh well, what the heck

Keep flirting with the taker; more than your soul is what he's after
He'll try to be bigger than your maker; you'll end up hanging from the rafter

So when he comes knocking, look him straight in the eye
And if he says, "Make a choice, do you live, or do you die?"

Think hard about your answer because the end is final
He'll nail the box shut and cover it with vinyl

But if you choose to stay, to see the light of tomorrow
Then tell the reaper to leave and find another soul to borrow

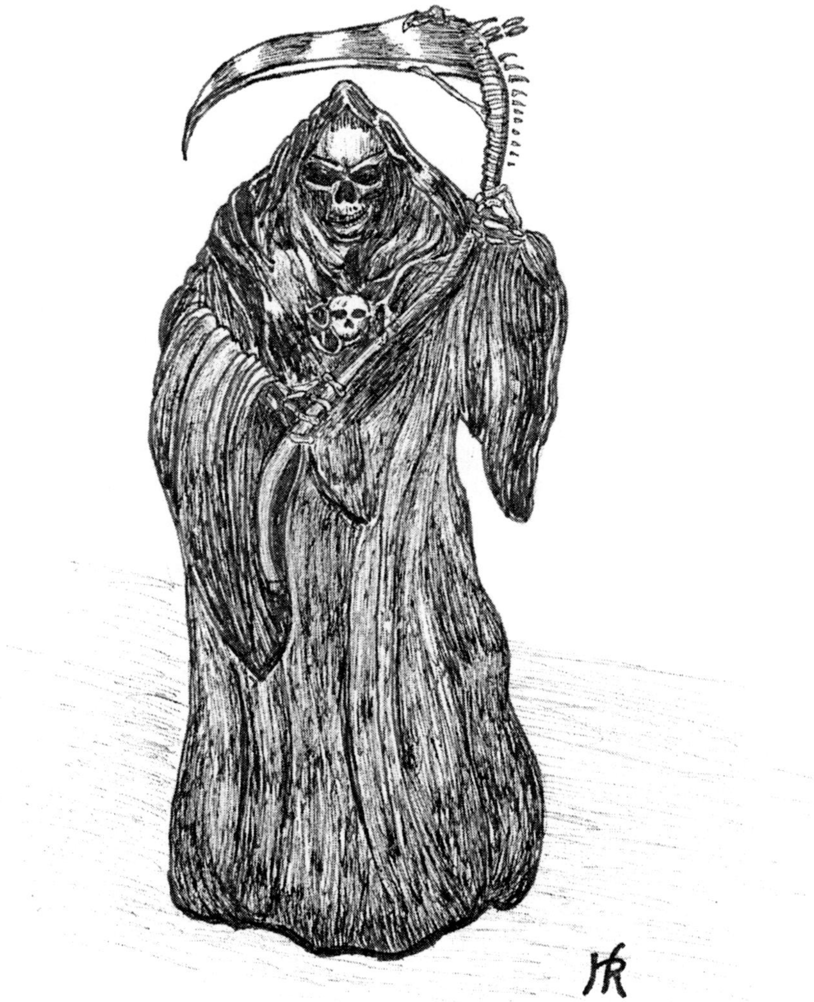

THE DEVIL

The circus came to town just the other day
Couldn't stand up straight; my body started to sway

Fast-moving lights, excitement all around
Felt right in my element, knew what I had found

Some called it the devil, said it'd cause a lot of pain
But I loved what it did, wanted to dance in the rain

Shooting pool with my friends; hey, the devil's in town
Let's go play some eight ball, or come to my crib—we'll get down

Put some chalk on your cue, rosin up your bow
Let's play the fiddle; he's your friend or your foe

Devil always plays his music when he gets to your house
Watch out for the alley cats; be quiet as a mouse

If you make too much noise, he might know you're afraid
And when he sees just that, in your grave you'll get laid

So heed my warnings; don't act like a clown
Just remember, beware when the devil's in town

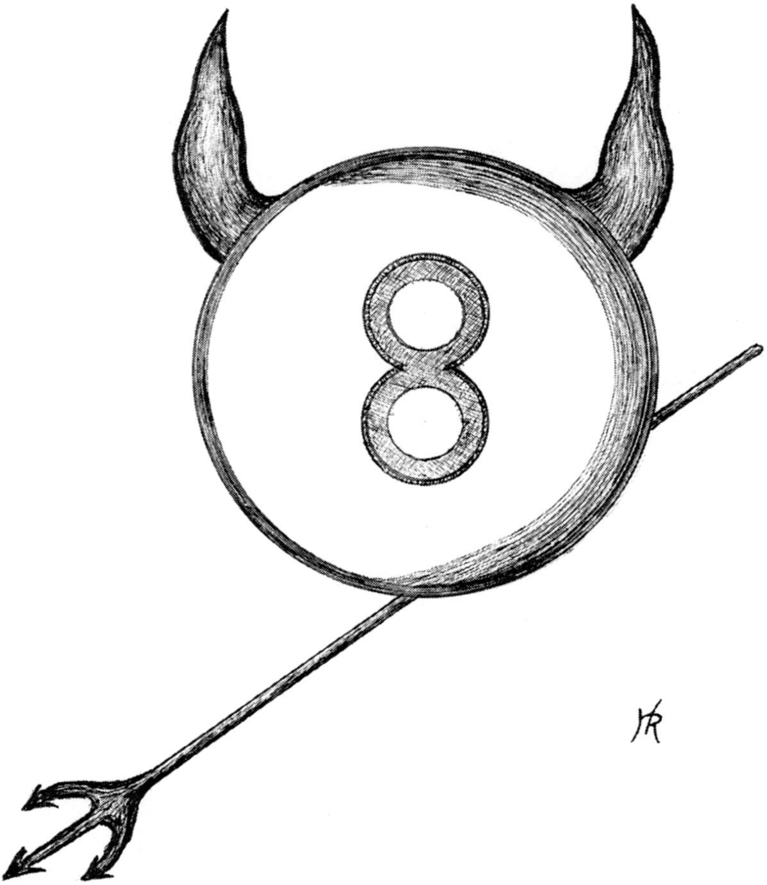
8

MARY JANE

I once had a friend named Mary Jane
I loved her dearly; I loved her name

She was the best friend that I ever had
She never got cross; she never got mad

Was always there to make my spirits high
When I was feeling down, she took me to the sky

Mary Jane and I were never apart
I loved what she did from the very start

We got introduced in '77
And right away, I was in heaven

I could never count how many albums we shared
And through thousands of movies, she was always there

We danced all night until the sun came up
She was right there beside me like a loyal little pup

As the end came near, she grew from a pup to a hound
Her affection and licks suddenly had me bound

Bound inside a deep paranoid state
Wouldn't answer the phone, wouldn't open the gate

I wanted to crawl and hide inside the drywall
The monster was coming, the fun time I couldn't recall

She turned on me quick; what happened to our love?
She became a hawk; she used to be a dove

A lot of time has passed, and it's better this way
My skies are filled with sun now when they used to be gray

But I'll always remember our first slow dance
When she became my lover and set me into a trance

And now it's time we say good-bye
I will miss my Mary; I will miss her high

BETWEEN THE LINES

Between the lines, I could not sleep
Between the lines, I started to weep

Between the lines, my heart stopped beating
Another day in the life that I had been cheating

Between the lines, I thought of death
I'm not Shakespeare, didn't write *Macbeth*

Between the lines, I took a break
My head was tired, couldn't stay awake

Between the lines, the nose started to drip
When the hell am I going to stop this trip?

Between the lines, I made a call
Gotta get on the ground, give me alcohol

Between the lines, brain's starting to melt
Can't feel anything, don't know what I felt

Between the lines, someone laid me to rest
I can't do this anymore, thought I did my best

Between the lines, it came to an end
Was feeling weak, think I'm starting to bend

Between the lines, I took some pills
They took me to bottoms and to the top of great hills

Between the lines, I decided to stop
Wanted my life back, had to become a rock

Between the lines, I asked to heal
Got it in twelve, turned over the wheel

Between the lines, I stopped for a look
I started to read from a different book

Out On A Cliff

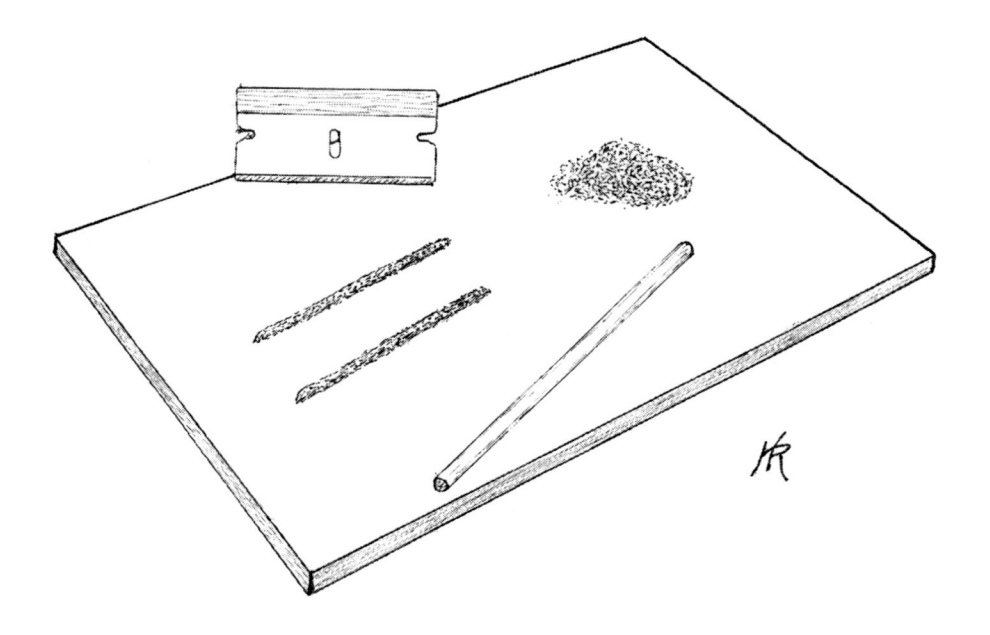

COMIN' DOWN

Gas in my gut, press real hard
Rumble in the hole, will I dump a shard?

In through the out door, blocked up real good
Pull out the branches, I'm barkin' wood

My eyes start to burn; my nose seals shut
Can't handle another minute of this pain in my gut

Why do I do it, chewin' Percs and morphine tabs?
Makes the pain disappear for a while, then starts the stabs

It's poor man's heroin, makes you wanna keep going
The side affects are bad; the heart keeps slowing

Was lucky once that the nurse came when she did
Heart stopped cold, could have landed on the skid

They used the paddles and electricity; the shock was huge
Thank God I'm alive; I was such a damn stooge

So I'd try the spike; maybe that's the trick
Chased the dragon down, but that made me sick

When I finally decided to clean out the junk
My body wouldn't cooperate, so I decided to get drunk

A few days later, everything started to shift
I could feel the change; what a lift

Out On A Cliff

Then with an explosion I empty; the blockage is gone
I coil out a Louisville Slugger that's twenty inches long

But for the week that follows, diarrhea is severe
I can't look at a pill or consider a beer

The pain of withdrawal was extreme, left me ill
Like rolling in barbwire and drinking bleach from a still

Now the pain is gone; I'm able to breathe
Clean towels and bedsheets, my god, what a relief

Getting clean is hell . . .

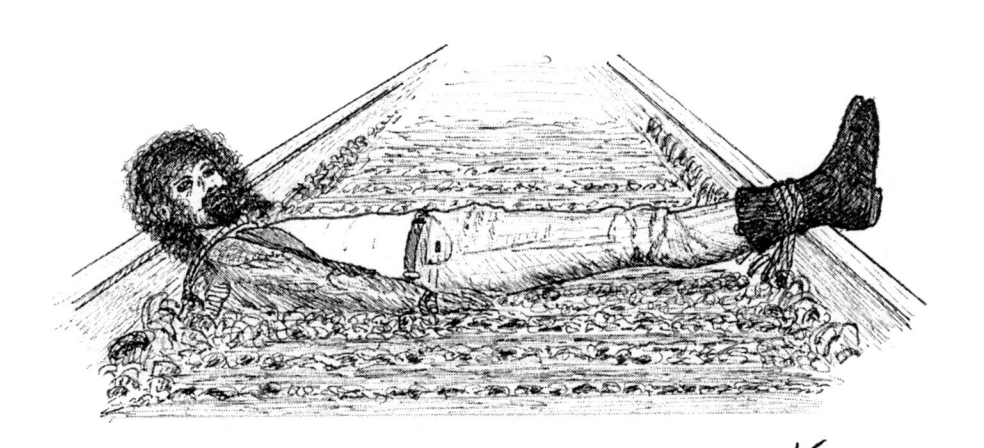

IN MY HEAD

In my head, I sometimes live
Do I take on too much? Do I have enough to give?

I used to have permanent residents living up there
Now they rent by the hour, and some of them share

So I try really hard, stay outta the place that's not fun
It's a dangerous space, all alone with no gun

The mind likes to race, like gerbils on a wheel
Sometimes it's so fast; don't know how I'm supposed to feel

Like the ramblings of a madman on the border of insane
Such a dangerous place, all alone in my brain

The path of destruction always starts with a thought
So be very careful; you could end up being shot

Deep inside of my head is where it begins
You'll end up losing, and nobody wins

So stay outta the darkness that lurks deep inside
But stay cool, keep it real; there's no need to hide

Out On A Cliff

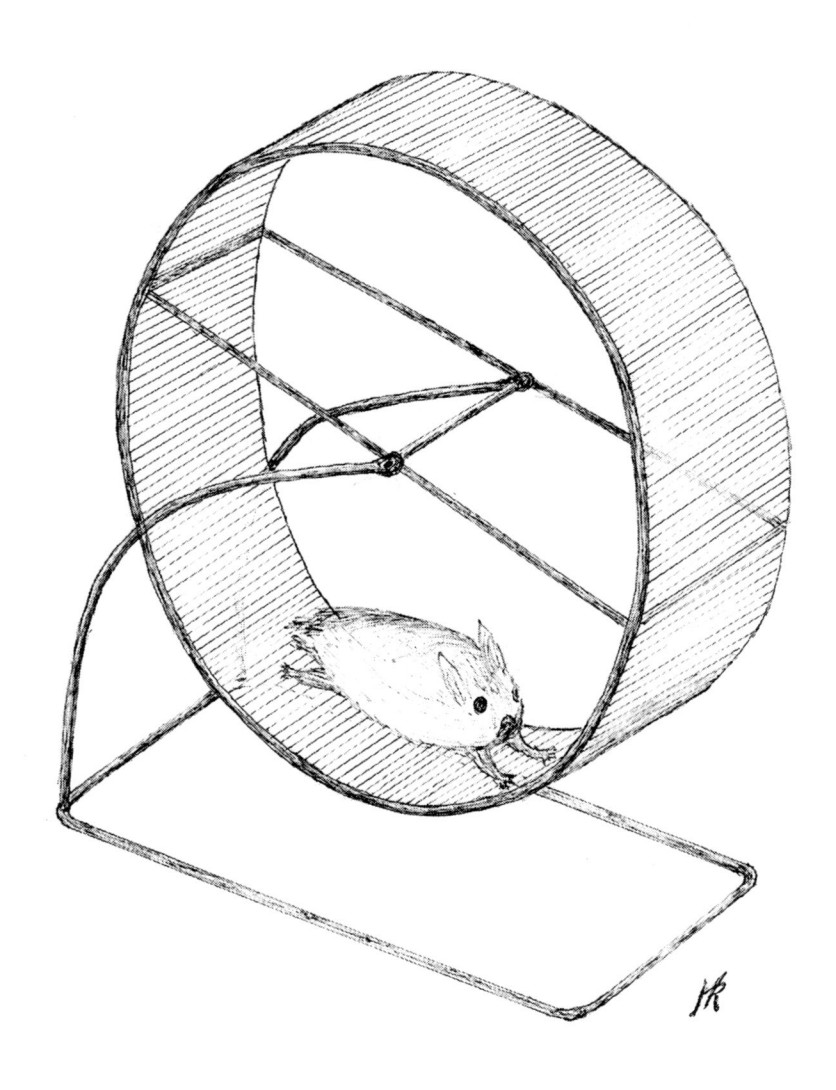

MY STRUGGLES

So you stumbled to the curb one last time
Leery to wind it up and share your last dime

Took another hit on the rock 'n' roll train
Hard to understand why you need this pain

You've crawled across the country on your hands and knees
Might as well join the circus, be part of the flyin' trapeze

It's a rotten feeling that sits in your gut
Are you completely insane or just kind of a nut?

Want that football inside to simply go away
Want to live clean for just one day

But as each sun rises and I'm on this side of the grass
I question out loud, when will my time pass?

When will I be taken from these flames of hell?
One day at a time, I'm supposed to get well

Yet the train sped along doing two hundred on the track
Better pull the rip cord, or there's no turning back

So I suffer, I cringe, and I occasionally binge
My life's on the line, hangin' on by a hinge

Out On A Cliff

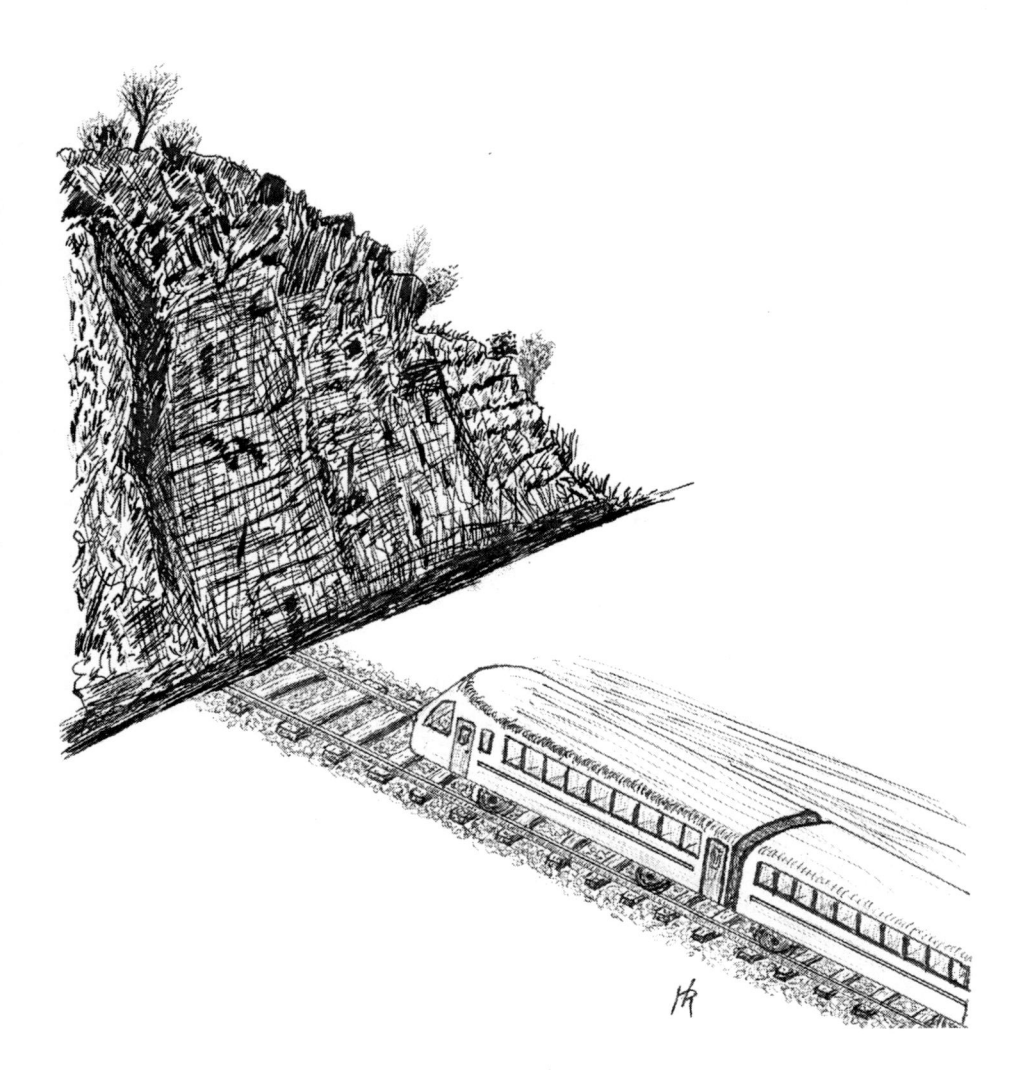

SELFISH

You've caused lots of pain and told many lies
Messed with their brains, heard all of their cries

You instilled fear and doubt; do you want it that way?
They're gonna lock you out, and they won't want to stay

They'd rather leave now; their hero is gone
Why did you do it, what went wrong?

Can't you keep it together? This game ain't that hard
Just whip yourself with leather; did life deal you a bad card?

You played spin the bottle one more time
Stole their trust, planted fear, said it would be fine

So keep moving forward; don't ever look back
Keep the train rolling steady; keep your wheels on the track

Look over your shoulder; you may turn to stone
Don't cross the border; you'll never be alone

Out On A Cliff

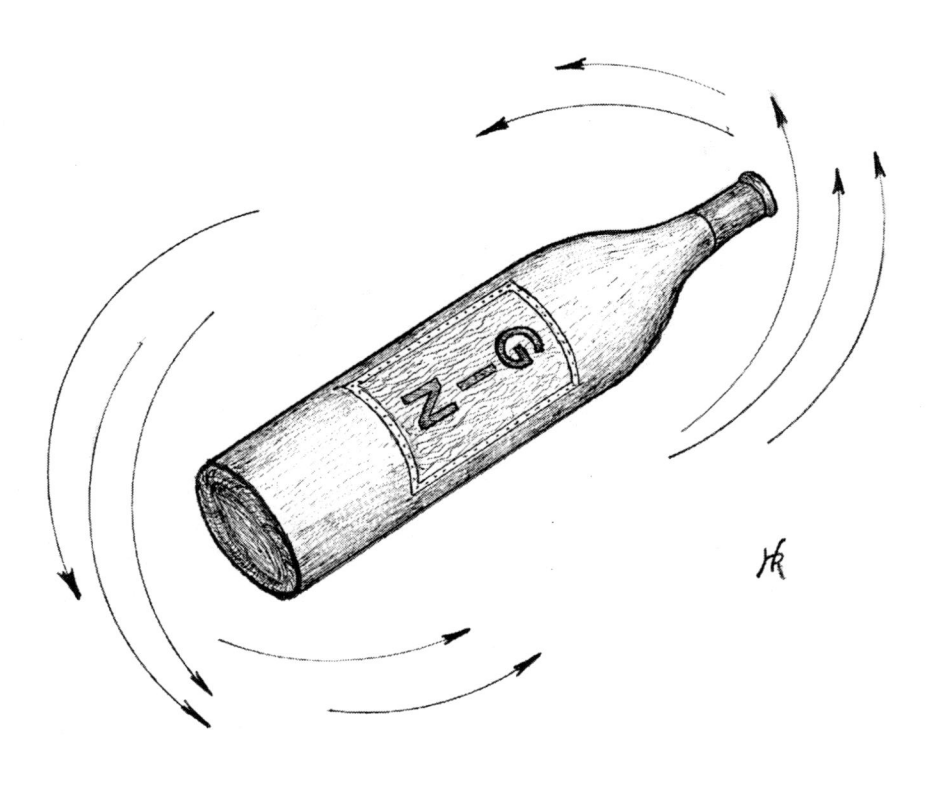

SWALLOWED UP

The crack in the ground flung open wide
No place to run, no place to hide

The crater got bigger with each step ahead
Maybe this is the time they'll find me dead

When 3:00 p.m. struck, the fuse got lit
Didn't matter what I had, just didn't give a shit

Was willing to lose my new life that was real
Just craved for the booze; didn't care how'd they feel

So I put myself out there on the edge by the drop
Didn't give a shit if I'd run into a cop

Run into a bunch is exactly what I did
Didn't run away, never ran, never hid

Self-sabotage is a game of sadness
No matter how good, you go back to the madness

Back to the pain 'cuz it's all that you know
I got nothing to gain, just feel so damn low

Then a moment of clarity slid through the big wall
And one by one, the bricks started to fall

A little bit of light broke over the top
And just like that, the insanity stopped

Another trip to hell I get to file away
Just thankful I'm alive to see one more day

Out On A Cliff

FGI

Sitting in the chair, waiting to be seen
Thinking about my friend Jim Beam

Cravings come, cravings go
I get so high, I get so low

The rush of getting to the next drink
Makes it so I can hardly think

Mind starts racing, head begins to sweat
Can't have one now, not now, not yet

Gotta go to the room and get my head clear
If I don't I'll end up with a gut full of beer

Wanna jump on a plane and go someplace hot
Bed down a cougar on my king-size cot

A week away is all I need
Although two would actually do the deed

Some R & R to clear my mind
Drink a few beers, see what I can find

I just need to go, get away from it all
If I don't get that chance, I may stumble and fall

Maybe what I need is a place to get clear
Forget the cougars, screw the beer

Someplace to walk and to write my story
In all its pain and all its glory

Dead man walking . . .

Out On A Cliff

ONE STEP, TWO

One step forward, two steps back
Tryin' hard to get well, tryin' to get on track

Working your recovery, then sliding into relapse
Makes all those small victories collapse

Why's it so hard to stay on the straight and narrow?
When some of the closest to you break your heart with an arrow

The sadness and shame you carry for letting them down
Is a burden so heavy in your chest, you see it in their frown

Their sad little faces, the tears in their eyes
Rip a hole through your soul; every fiber in you cries

And the one you love the most. she stands by your side
So you gotta pull your shit together, can't run and hide

There's a cosmic connection between her and I
Venus meets Mars and becomes one in the sky

Whatever their differences, they are just meant to be
God put them together from now till eternity

She walked in cold; she didn't have a clue
What the next insane step was; she didn't know what I'd do

Some of it was laughable, some very tense
But she always stayed close, never rode the fence

Out On A Cliff

She's all I have now; I shamed the little ones away
I pray in my heart that they'll come back one day

I fight through anxiety, with my lady and me
God handed her off; she knew where to be

She seemed to understand and certainly accepted her new role
I can never repay her, except with all my love and a piece of my soul

One step forward, two steps back
Tryin' hard to get well, tryin' hard to get on track

VENUS   EARTH   MARS

WHAT I SEE
(PEDDLERS ON THE BEACH)

Waves on the beach crash upon the ground
Mind racing elsewhere of a love I have found

Sailboats are gently gliding through the big blue ocean
Bodies line the sand, glistening with lotion

Pelicans soar and parasailors fly
Staring at the sun and the clear, cloudless sky

Peddlers selling silver and handmade guitars
Tourists drinking sodas and beers at the bars

Hey, gringo, you like? I make it myself
If you don't buy, it goes back on the shelf

Maybe you like to party, I got green and some white
Will take you through the day and well into the night

Perhaps you like my lady, one thousand pesos—she's yours
I come from a family of drug dealers and whores

Okay, just relax, sit back in your chair
If I don't have it here, I can get it from there

So you like my product? You tell all of your friends?
If they buy from me also, I will please you to no ends

Okay, my friend, now I leave you alone
In twenty-four hours, you gonna fly home

Out On A Cliff

LINES ON MY FACE

Mirror, mirror on the wall
If I look and you crack, will I then fall?

Crumble to the ground because of what I've seen
The haunting past of where I've been

Lines on my face are clear . . . tell a story
Of a time in my life when the party was the glory

Lines that carry a million tales
A face full of scars; each scar has a trail

A full life lived by such a young man
Skin of pale, no time for a tan

Tanning is a slow and relaxing process
I simply burned, and then I'd regress

Each time I tried to take the better road
I'd end back on the one with the code

And again a new line would appear on my face
Maybe one day I'll take myself out of the race

But for now I fight the battle within
Then more lines appear, some thicker some thin

Out On A Cliff

40-40

So there I sat in my black leather chair
Basement apartment, all alone down there

Self-pity is a dangerous place in my head
Depression so dark, I wished I was dead

How far down could I possibly go?
Getting older each day; time doesn't pass slow

What's at the end, do I really wanna find out?
Feel so low and worthless; I grind, scream and shout.

Today's a special day; brought home toys to have some fun
A big bottle of vodka to take some of the pain, fix the rest with my gun

Smith & Wesson .40 caliber semiauto will stop the pain
Forty ounces of Iceberg Vodka to take me outside of my brain

I was at the point of no return
Taking off to the promised land, there was nothing left to learn

The very thing that was killing me saved my life that night
You see, I'm a blackout drinker, didn't pull the trigger, woke up all right

Loaded semiauto on my lap, bottle of Iceberg on the floor
At first I was pissed, failed plan, needed to think a little more

So a big gulp of Iceberg helped to clear the pounding mind
Put the gun on the coffee table, what am I trying to find?

A few years have crept behind me since that very dark day
So today I'm very grateful that God let me stay

The addict's mind is such a dangerous place to be
Stay out of that darkness and try to live shameless and guilt-free

The mass of men lead lives of quiet desperation ~ (Henry David Thoreau)

Out On A Cliff

Gary Rubie and Henk Rubie

ON THE EDGE OF THE CLIFF

Drove my truck to the edge of the cliff; the bottom did not look back
Don't get too close, may slip and fall, life slipping through the cracks

Is this the way I wanted to go, a coward in the end?
Or do I want to fix all my wrongs and try to make amends?

Had yellow rope inside my truck; there were some trees nearby
But did I want my cowboy boots to swing, did I want to hang 'em high?

I could head back home, eat a jar of pills—I got enough on hand
Take a few hundred, chase it with booze; it won't be an ugly end

Since I gave up my .40 caliber,
that option wasn't as easy and added a question mark
I know the right people and could get a Saturday
night special then do it in the park

It's three days to Christmas; it'd be one they'd never forget
The hardened side of me says no, they won't win,
I'm not ready to split just yet

So I grind my teeth, shake in my sleep, have to practice faith and patience
Body feels different, mind's not right,
everything's changed; it happened in an instance

What's God's plan for me?
They say he never gives you more than you can handle
But my cup is overflowing, my bathtub's flooded; Jesus Christ,
what did I do to earn this bundle?

I know there's much to be grateful for
Can't push everyone away; gotta let them through the door

Every move I make has to be calculated and safe
I can't let the PTSD cause me to make a sudden mistake

I've made a few that I can't get back
Gotta get on a new path and stay on track

Out On A Cliff

I'm getting hit from six different sides, I feel myself falling
Just wanna go run and hide, curl up and start bawling

Doctor says go away for a month and leave it all back here
I wanna go, but I don't know where, feel I might have to shed a tear

LOSE IT

I was walking out; you were walking in
Just the sight of you made the hair stand on my skin

We started together; I always stayed one of the boys
You climbed hard, crushing others, making noise

Did you find your gold watch? Was it hidden up tight?
Did you enter the darkness where there is no light?

I saw the bottom of your shoes hanging out of the chief's ass
You may have three ranks, but you got no class

We exchanged unpleasantries, and you pushed the right buttons
With a head full of meds, couldn't control my reactions

The rage that I spewed, it was covered with spit
Your arrogant, cocky look turned to worry, thought you'd shit

When I finally got a grip and realized what I was doing
A crowd started to gather; I knew I had to get going

Made it most of the way home, then got lit up
Looked like three cruisers were trying to get me to stop

It's not really a chase if you cruise the speed limit
But the boys weren't impressed, and when I stopped, they showed it

A couple to the head and ribs, and a knee to the thigh
Finally, one said, "He's one of us, I know this guy"

Got cautioned for cause, failure to stop, and road rage
I was so lucky that night; I didn't end up in a cage

Feels like I stepped back on any progress I made
My frustration is mounting; my anxiety is frayed

So Dr. Freud added Ritalin to help slow things down
I'm on so many meds, I feel deflated, like I've drowned

Out On A Cliff

Gary Rubie and Henk Rubie

LAST WALTZ

Drove into Brampton to get me a gun
Couldn't find what I wanted, decided I'd run

With booze in hand, I headed west for the lake
Gonna swim right across it, knew what's at stake

Meds in my head, a tonne of booze in my gut
Do I leave a legacy of a fuckup and a nut?

I crossed every line and boundary that was set
I had hit my wall, simply didn't give a shit

Couldn't break through the wall of mortar and brick
To me life was over, was a failure and a prick

You see, I built the wall long ago deep in my head
It was how I protected myself; if I hadn't, I'd be dead

But now was the time for the last waltz; I knew I had to go
Weigh the hurt I'd leave behind against fixing what I know

When I got to the pier and was ready to swim,
my mind suddenly turned around
Can't do the swim; God, help me through this, take me home to my town

But that wasn't to be; I was digging a new hole deeper into the ground
God taught me a lesson, a new low now found

While driving in a blackout, my lady told me I needed to stop
When I told her I was bigger than God, she called an OPP cop

The next thing that I remember was waking in a jail cell
Had I killed someone? What had happened? Was this the last waltz in hell?

I had fought the good fight; now I've finished the race
Signed myself out and found strength to face the disgrace

What a low, what a bottom; IA's coming for the ride
What have I done? I'm so ashamed, want to run and hide

Out On A Cliff

Time to man up and face the devil; the dance is over
All those years I cheated the system; now I wear the four-leaf clover

No one died, but I got injured and still feel the sting
The song is over, the music stopped; I no longer want to sing

Bought myself round 3 in treatment
Keep an open mind, bury the resentment

Patience and faith until the legal battles end
Get back my badge and allow my broken body to mend

The history of trauma is complete; the hard part is done
Time to let my head heal; the whole process cost me a tonne

But now was the time for the last waltz; I knew I couldn't go
I weighed the hurt I'd leave behind, decided to fix what I know

It's Over.

Gary Rubie and Henk Rubie

SEGREGATION

The gates slammed shut; I'd done it now, this time it was for real
Bail denied, come back in five days; hey, tough guy, how's it feel?

This time was different, no talking my way out
Every fiber of fear inside wanted to scream and shout

I was going to be inside the cage, not gonna be the guy looking in
Bed of concrete, doors of steel, my head was starting to spin

Stripped down naked inside the jail
Seen the evidence of their beating on my skin; don't dare make a wail

Stripped of every personal belonging; bend over, touch your toes
Pride, self-respect, and dignity got packed up with my clothes

Put on the orange jumpsuit and blue runners, buttercup
You ain't fuck-all in here, cop, so mouth closed and keep it shut

There are 1,300 like you locked up in their cages
Each with their own story, each with their own rages

But we're gonna protect your ass; for you it's segregation
You'll be locked alone for 24-7; it'll save you from damnation

The boys wanna cut you up something bad
Don't whimper, don't cry; there's no running home to your Dad

Do your time clean, don't cause no shit
Behave yourself; you'll get out sooner, then you can suck on your mommy's tit

Sorry your cage is now occupied; gotta move you someplace new
One nigger stabbed a brother, so now he's got
your cell; there's nothing we can do

If you cause us grief, you'll go to the hole, and you thought this place was bad
All alone and in the dark, animals chew you; you'll remember what you had

Out On A Cliff

Time passed slowly; I prayed each day, bail hearing put off again
And then it happened—I made my bail on a short leash;
never going back to the den

Tight conditions, twenty-four-hour supervision,
back to treatment for ninety days
It beats the hell out of where I was in oh so many ways

Someone . . . anyone . . . help . . .

MY FRIEND (LANGER)

Picked up the phone and made the call
Help was finally on its way
He dropped everything; he dropped it all
A true friend was here to stay

When he arrived, I spoke for hours
He listened quietly with nothing to say
The tears ran down like showers
Help arrived from the west that day

Then my friend started to speak
His words were gentle, kind, and serene
All my fiber had become so weak
He knew exactly where I had been

He had walked this path before
The journey would be long and slow
Another brought him to the door
As he showed me the way to go

He led me to the room
The door swung open wide
I was swept in, like the dust on a broom
Thank God I had finally arrived

The meeting ended quickly
Not remembering a word being said
A warm welcome along with a handshake
Joy and happiness filled my head

Take me to another meeting, my dear friend
I don't want this feeling to go away
A state of happiness I never wanted to end
Don't let me ever again go astray

Out On A Cliff

Many years have gone since that day
My friend still lives by action
Many stories we have shared along the way
If I could only be as pure by a fraction

A true friend like this comes but once
A life owed by a brother gone astray
You're my best friend, a brother, a confidant
My payback is clean living day by day

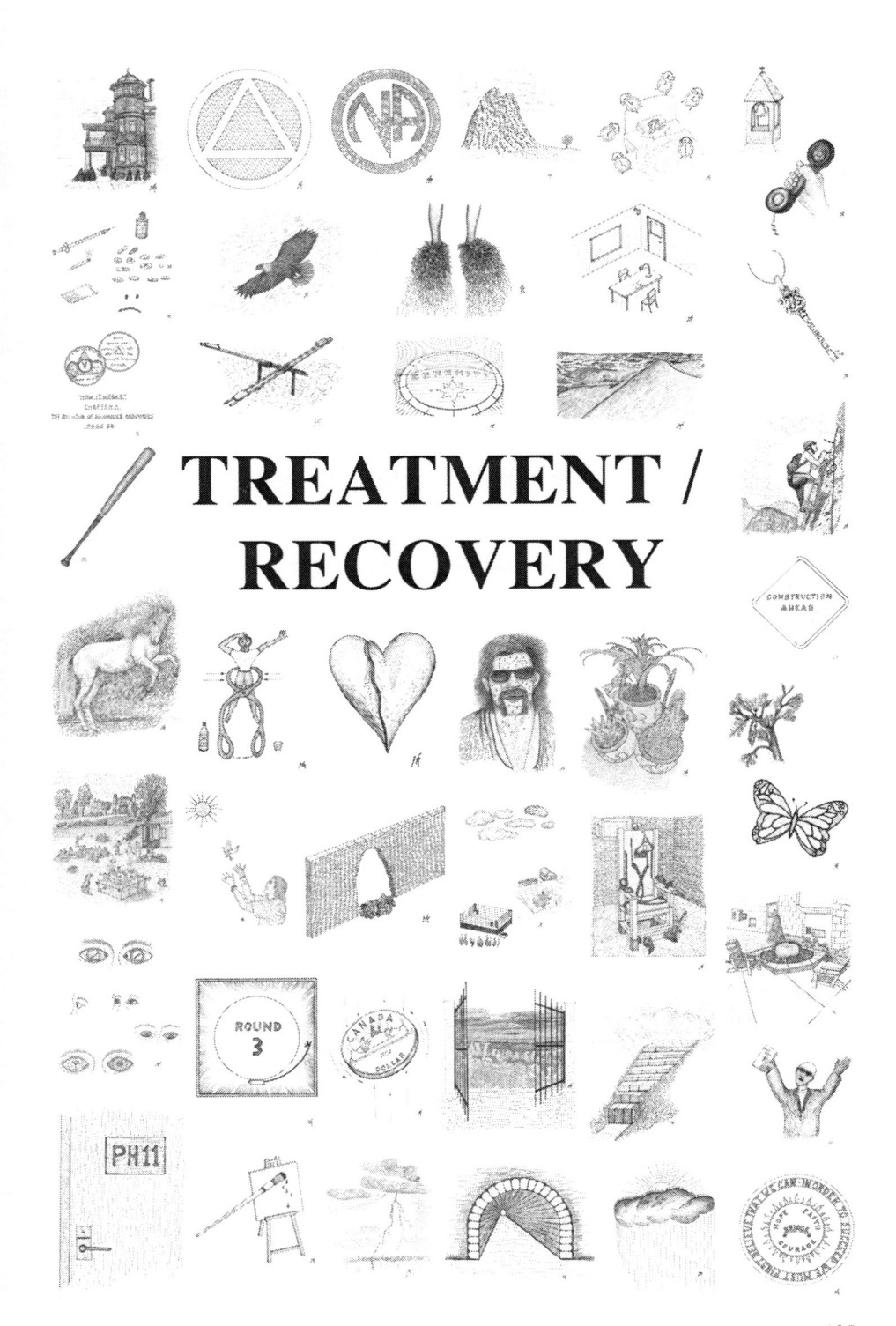

TREATMENT / RECOVERY

TREATMENT

Sittin' here in treatment, feeling lots of shame
Pointed my fingers, but knew I was to blame

I was the one that destroyed all those lives
Took a few dozen hostages and a couple of wives

A wake of disaster was left in my path
There wasn't enough whiskey to fill up my bath

My tub was big, held thousands of liters
Crashed a few cars, drove a few beaters

Wanna turn it around, gotta make things right
Live clean every day and into the night

Don't run with the devil; that'll take me to hell
Hang with the winners, and all will be well

Out On A Cliff

TAKING THAT STEP

I walked through the door, shoulders slumped down
Couldn't crack a smile, only knew how to frown

Wanted to get well, wanted the pain to go away
Did the three-month program; knew I had to stay

The price was great; my daughter moved out
We used to talk to each other; now all we do is shout

I was once a brilliant chalice that got shattered on the ground
But others didn't see me as broken; instead, shiny pieces they had found

They loved me unconditionally, something I simply couldn't do
When the strength to love came back, I learned to love me too

I still fight with the devil that lurks deep within
Gotta keep moving forward, can't let the devil win

He sits on my shoulder, does push-ups all day
Waiting for me to weaken, waiting for me to sway

Got seven weeks to go; just one day at a time
Stay strong, keep it simple, and all will be fine

IN ORDER TO SUCCEED WE MUST FIRST BELIEVE THAT WE CAN

HOPE · FAITH · BRIDGE · COURAGE

THE HOLE

So much fury, so much pain, so much anger in my brain
So much lost
Nothing gained
The hatred rages on again

Have no love
Have no hope
The only thing I have is dope

Everything gone
So much to lose
My whole damn life was fueled by booze

Morning shakes
Morning dries
Nothing good
No more highs

Chasing the dragon
Again and again
Had me caged
Within a pen

Money made
Money gone
Singing that same old
Tragic song

Another life
Flushed down the drain
Everything to lose
Nothing to gain

Hit the bottom
Bounced back up
Learned to drink
From a different cup

OUT ON A CLIFF

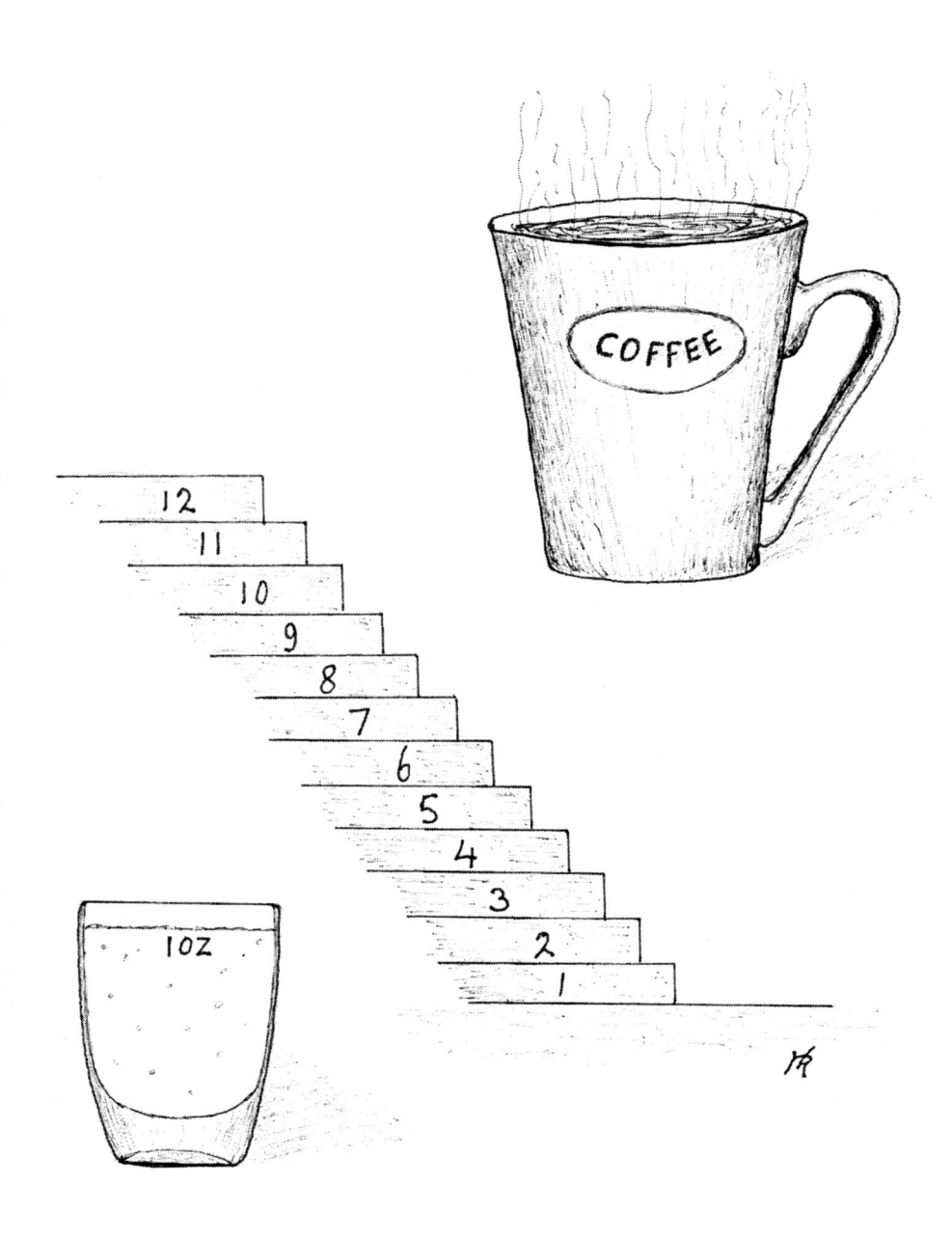

STORM

As I fell out of the clouds
My head broke through the rains
The lightning cracked so loud
Turned the blood cold in my veins

What I didn't see was so damn clear
Starin' me right in the face
Been foggy for so many a year
Turned my life into a bitter disgrace

I saw the sadness in their eyes
Was I the cause of all this pain?
My heart broke, and I started to cry
Can't take them through this storm again

Asked my maker to take me home
Said my time wasn't over just yet
He promised to never let me alone
Taking the journey together step-by-step

Found a better way of life
There was much left for me to do
Happiness replaced the strife
Grateful for the storm I walked through

Out On A Cliff

ALPHA ROOM

We sit around the table's square
Sometimes here, sometimes there

Empty out your bag of pain
Then you choose to take some home again

Telling strangers just how you feel
Sometimes none of it seems to be real

Work your program, tell the truth
Watch the survivors; they're living proof

Get a sponsor, don't take the first drink
One thing's for sure: the program makes you think

Take a chip for desire; get the power that's higher
Every now and then, you'll run into a liar

Live your life by twelve simple rules
Hang with the winners, stay away from the fools

Keep it simple, one day at a time
Live a clean life, and all will be fine

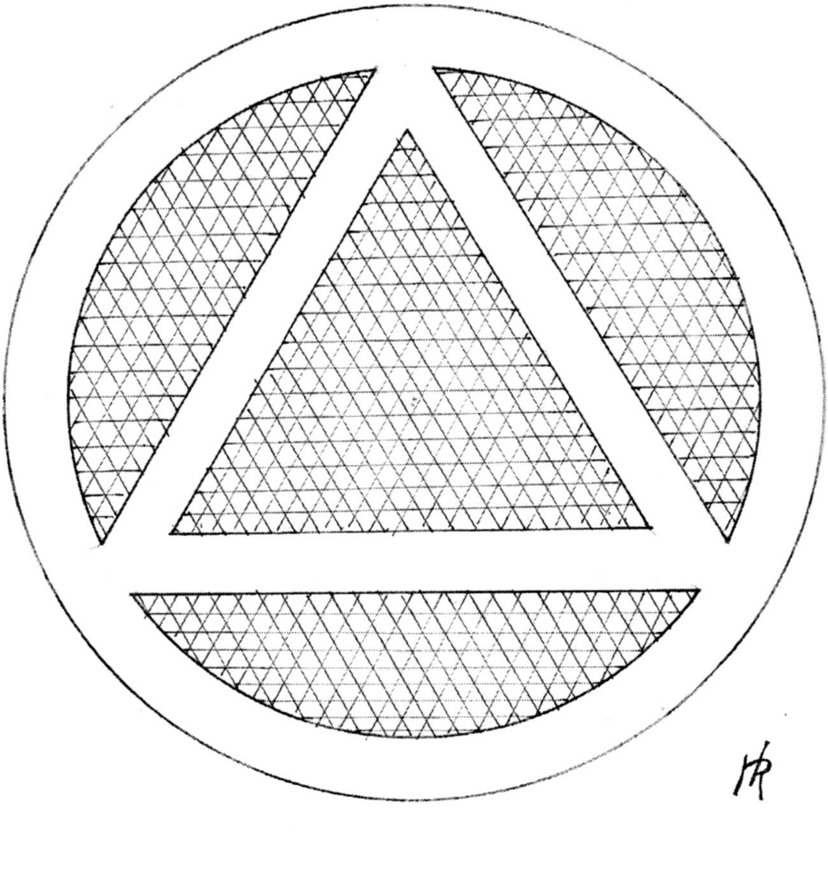

CLOSED N.A.

Sitting in a circle, sharin' what I think
Some here for drugs, some 'cuz of the drink

Every story's different; everyone's the same
Each disaster changes, but they all end in pain

For some the pain's great, stretching far—stretching wide
Went through their own hell; some even tried suicide

My story's no different; I dug my own grave
Using would cause death; recovery would save

So I checked into the "home"; they treat all kinds
Help mend broken bodies and insane minds

It doesn't matter what you took or how high you got
We're all travelling the same road; know we're in the right spot

So we share what we feel with complete, total strangers
A plumber, a roofer, a doctor, even park rangers

And when the meeting's over, we take what we need
Remembering to avoid seedy people and that skunky green weed

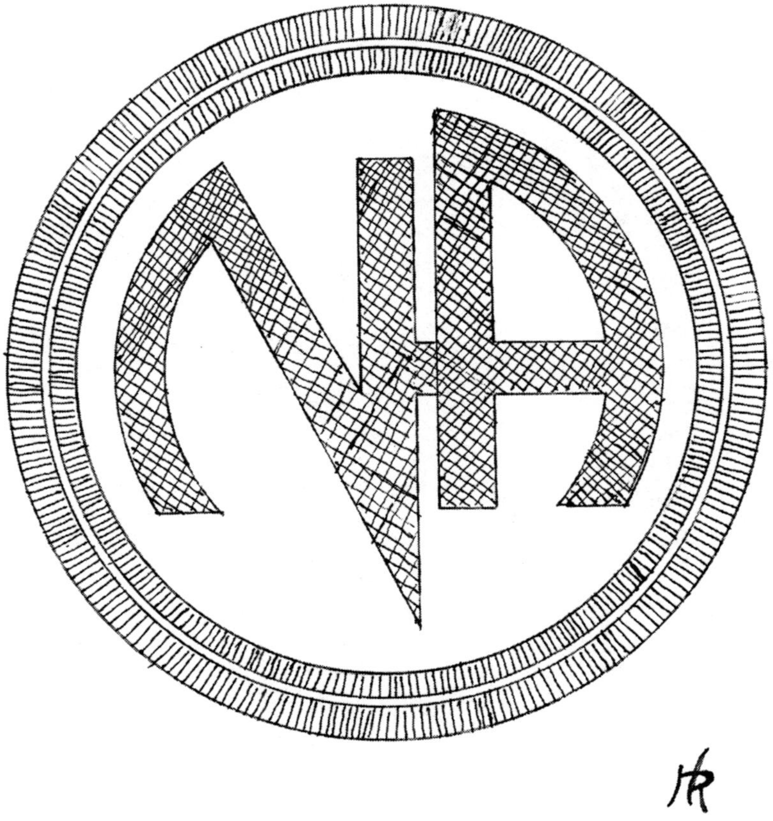

THE CIRCLE

What a gift I've been given, second chances received
It's a miracle I'm alive; so hard to believe

All the yesterdays are gone; they will never return
So I gotta stop living there, just take the lessons that I learned

Tomorrow's not here, and it may never come
So I try and keep it in the moment; that's where there's fun

Remember, today's the present, so it's truly a gift
Through your day, think of this often, and it will give you a lift

Isn't life just wonderful, having family to love?
Be sure to be thankful for that gift from above

I can't thank God enough for where my life has gone
Because the hell that I endured will help another get strong

Yes, I'm grateful for all the suffering, the losses, and the hurt
One day I will help rebuild a broken man, and then he will wear my shirt

And so the circle goes; it's special just for us
The circle of recovery, with humility and little fuss

Not every day is a bed of roses, but it's a lot better than it was
When I lived my life in yesterday, full of resentment and loss

"HOW IT WORKS"

CHAPTER 5

THE BIG BOOK OF ALCOHOLICS ANONYMOUS

PAGE 58

STEP UP TO THE PLATE

Step up to the plate, take a swing
Round the bases, do your thing

Crank it hard, send it to the sky
Don't know how long you'll live or when you'll die

Hit a single, safe at first
Or you hit a double; it could be worse

You hit a triple, slide into the dirt
Be a real man; you don't wear a skirt

Then once in a while, when things don't seem fun
You step up to the plate, and you belt a home run

And when that happens, and everything's great
You won't be afraid to step up to the plate

Out On A Cliff

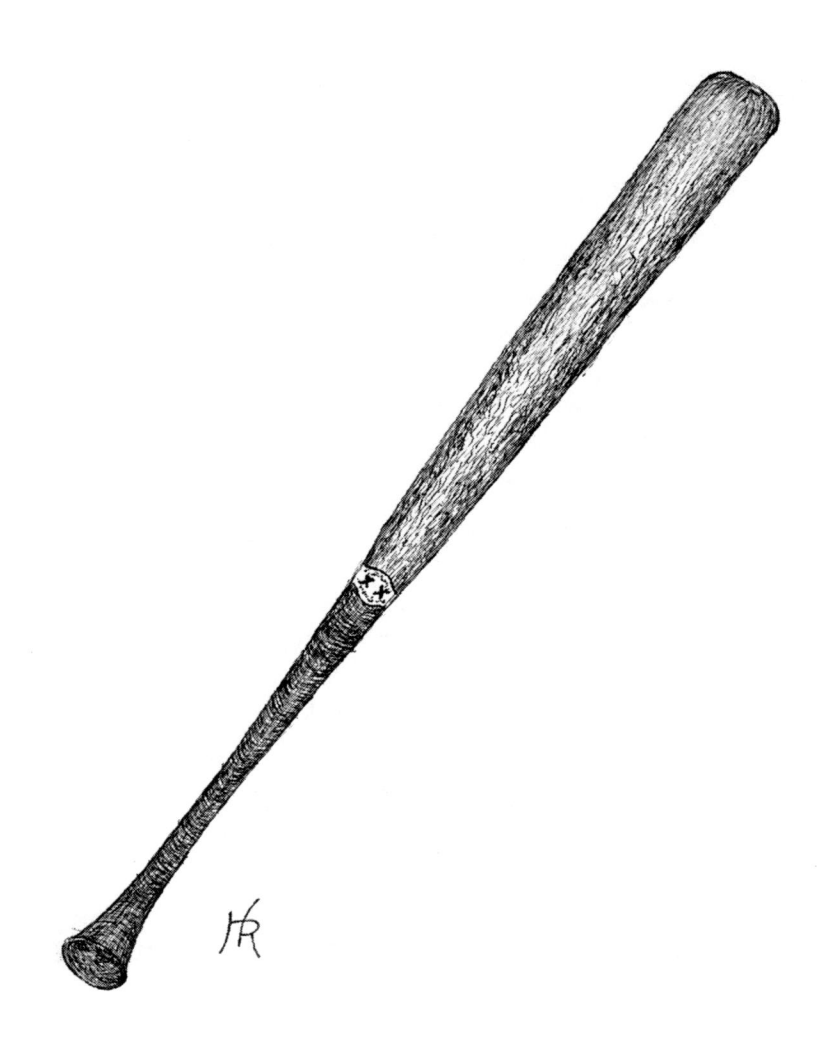

BALANCE AND STRUCTURE

Balance and structure have not yet been found
It's so hard to get to that middle ground

People pleasing from the moment I get home
Don't have any time to be on my own

My kids push hard; they're starving for love
But the way they go about it ain't with a kid glove

They use what they know, manipulation and guilt
Feel like I'm falling off a stilt

I openly question my skills as a dad
Doing the best that I can, but I still feel sad

It sometimes overwhelms; that sadness and pain
I'm caught in a storm, and I can't stop the rain

The rain and the pain seem to follow my life
I can't blame my kids, can't blame my ex-wife

Even with their sharp tongues that can cut like a knife
That adds to my pain and causes me strife

I gotta stay real for no one but me
If I stumble and fall, I'll kill the family tree

I'm trying so hard to keep it all together
Don't know if I can battle any more stormy weather

So I'm giving it away, up to my higher power
I pray every day, sometimes every hour

So I'll listen real close to hear that quiet voice
And I know that he will guide me to make the right choice

Out On A Cliff

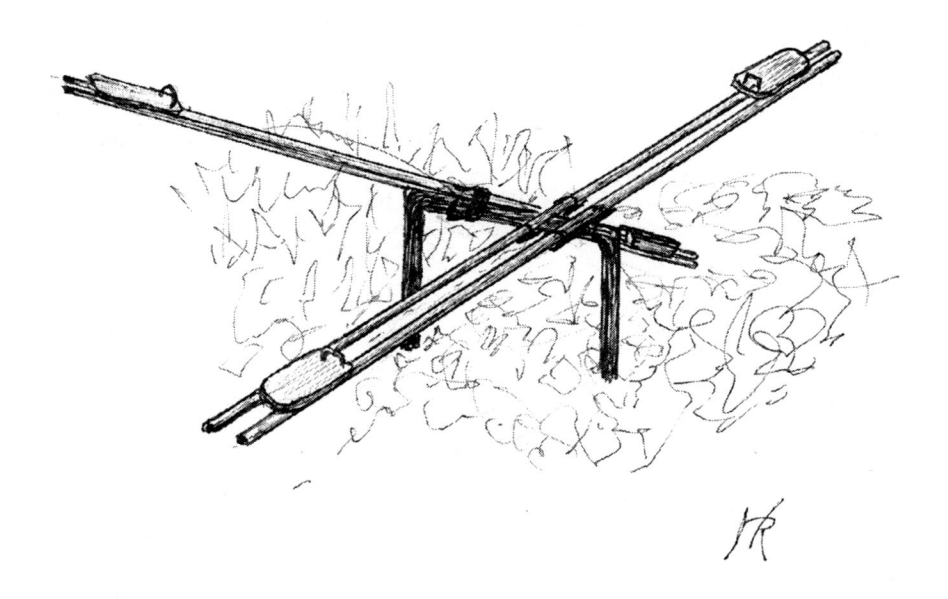

P.V. MEXICO

Got off the plane, could feel the heat
Slow down my life, slow down my feet

Sweat hits my brow, heart's still racing like crazy
Where am I right now? I need to try and get lazy

It's hard to slow down when you go this fast
I think everyone knows that your heart just won't last

So you make an effort; you know it will work
You've been here before; you've had this quirk

It's all about control; I keep taking it back
If I'm not real careful, will end up on a rack

So I look at the sun, and when day turns to night
I'm feeling more mellow, really love the sight

The stars make me think, the moon makes me crazy
If I pull an all-nighter, I'll end up pushing the daisies

Then the sun comes up just one more time
I awake to the heat, know I'm feeling just fine

So I'm graced once again; I'm alive on my feet
The good Lord has allowed me to enjoy this heat

As I walk along the dark sandy beach
Feeling all right, eyes don't need the bleach

So it took a few days, but I've slowed it right down
Enjoy my stay, and don't act like a clown

Me and my kin hangin' tough to the end
Don't go to the bar, don't sway, don't bend

Out On A Cliff

STRANGLEHOLD

I'm in the grip of something so strong
When will it end? Please tell me how long

The grip is a continuing and progressive illness
For all of it to stop, I need to find the willingness

I know that the end will always be the same
Jails, institutions, or death with great shame

A lot is my choice, the rest is disease
Have to take it real slow, keep my life at ease

I slip into darkness every now and then
I never know when it happens, just don't know when

The feelings, they scare me, like I could suddenly break
So they fill me with meds; they all know what's at stake

I've slipped back to a place that's full of rage
Sometimes I wonder if I'd be better off in a cage

Outbursts that happen without warnings or signs
Those moments are scary 'cuz I end up cryin'

I want to go back to the feelings of calm
I can't go on erupting like a ticking time bomb

I scare everyone around, including myself
I don't like how that feels, want it put on a shelf

They call this recovery, but my frustration is great
I have to listen to God, listen to my innate . . .

Out On A Cliff

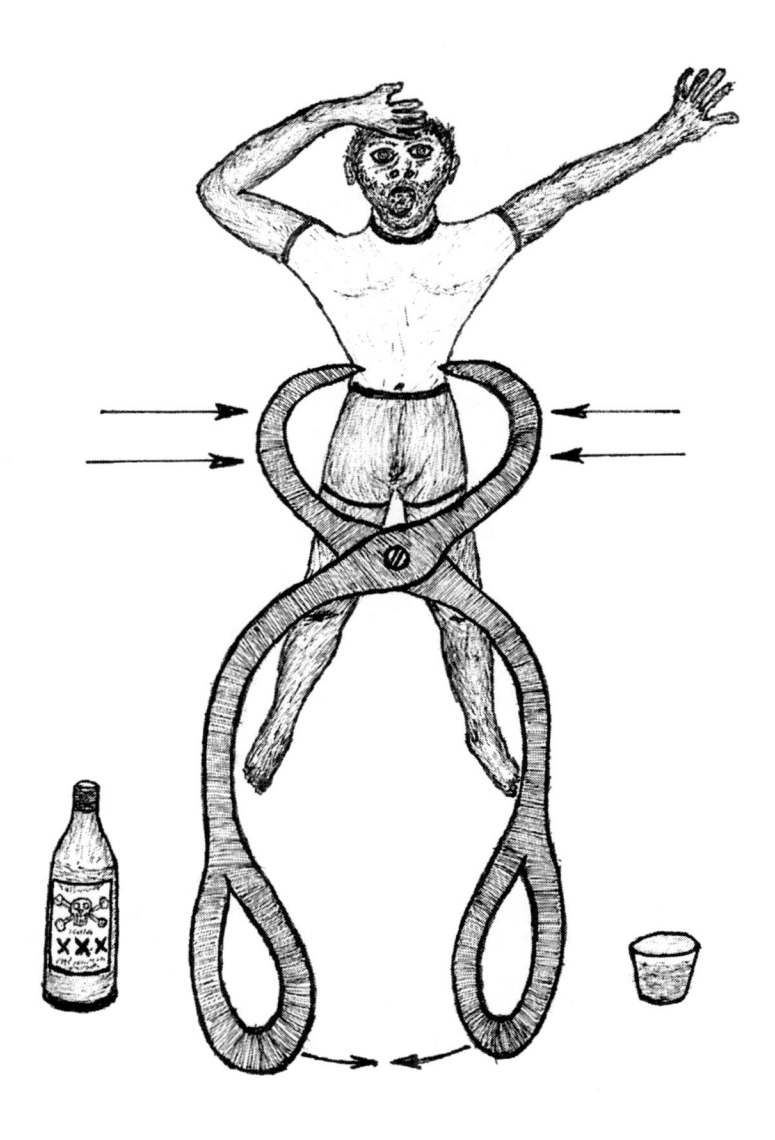

ANXIETY

Hands are sweaty, feet are cold
Mind is racing, can't get a hold

Body shaking like a leaf
Can't find the answer, can't find my relief

Been searching so long to get it straight
How the hell do I get to the pearly gate?

Maybe Dante's *Inferno* is where I'll go
But I've been there before; hell, I just don't know

Slipping up the icy mountain
to get a taste from the golden fountain

I get halfway there, and I slide back up
always drinking from different cup

So I dig in hard with the claws on my shoes
Trying to run from the evil booze

Like the great magnetic rock, far in the north
A compass won't let me follow the course

So I add new claws to my hands and knees
Crawling up the mountain to find my peace

And if I find it, I'll surely know
There is no better place to go

Out On A Cliff

EYES

The eyes tell the story of happiness or strife
They're black like tombstones, holding on to a knife

Sometimes they smile and look so alive
Other times they sting, like the bees in a hive

So we alter their looks with colors and inks
Or put in the contacts or change them with drinks

Champagne eyes wear the cloth of pain
The more booze you pour in them, the redder the vein

But every set of eyes is the gateway to the soul
If you look close enough, you'll see if life took its toll

Some eyes have the million-mile stare
They look right through you, like you're not even there

As the years go by and the wisdom grows
The eyes start to mellow; they let go of their foes

Getting to that point takes an awful lot of pain
As the end draws near, you finally get what you gained

Then a calm, cool happiness is what everyone feels
When they look into the eyes that were once made from steel

Out On A Cliff

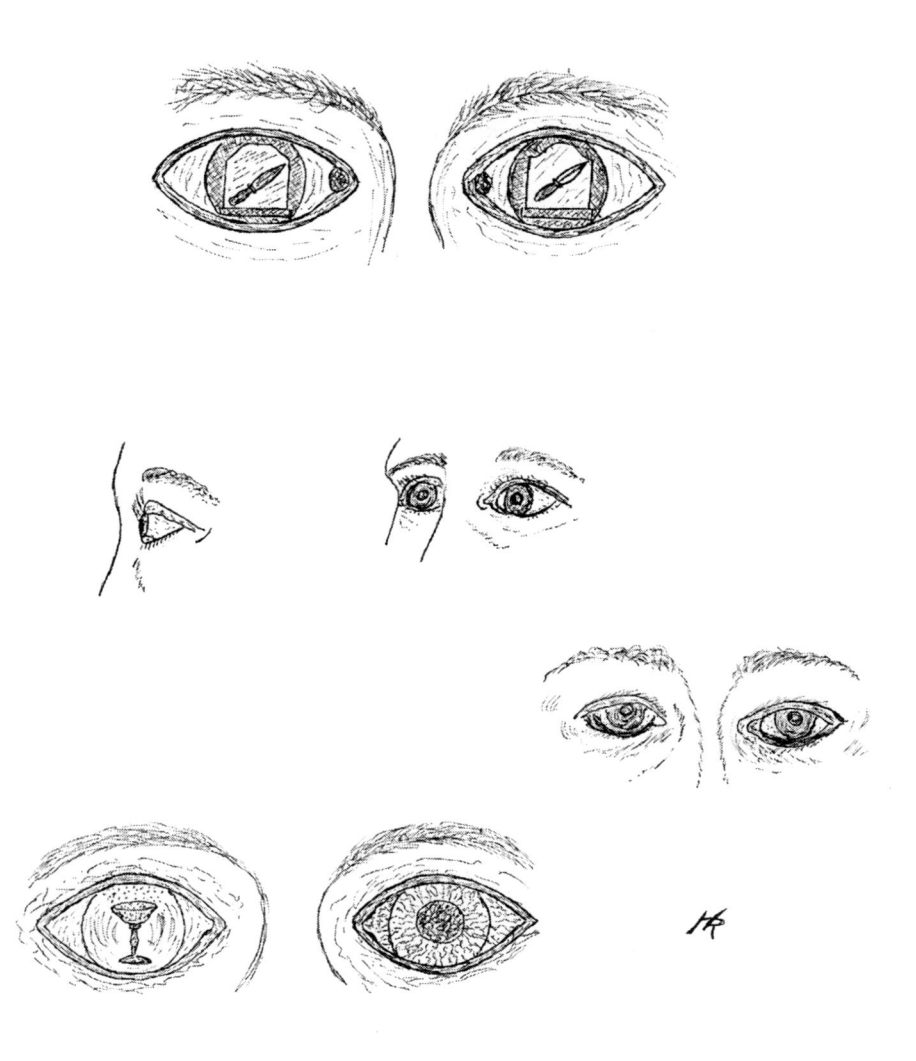

2009

It's Christmas Day 2009; a year has come and gone
Three hundred sixty-five very long days, I've managed to stay clean this long

A year ago on Christmas Day, I hosted my family for turkey
The day went by, and I remember very little;
the memories are vague and murky

It's been a long year with so many changes
Not all have been easy; they've come in stages

I asked for help, so I went away; four months alone in the home
Two different programs, five disorders, got treated in the big house of stone

When they let me out, I got a new doctor to crawl inside my head
He specialized in pharmaceutical psychology; he assured me I wasn't dead

I was overmedicated and just didn't feel; thought my life had come to an end
The doctor said not to worry; he'd balance my moods,
and then I'd be on the mend

He's been treating me for six months now;
it seems we've tinkered with every med
My frustration and depression go through the roof;
some days I just wanna stay in bed

I need to find a purpose in life to get me out of the door
Go to the gym, volunteer work, not pacing on the floor

They say the road to recovery is always under construction
So I have to keep moving forward 'cuz the past was full of destruction

CONSTRUCTION
AHEAD

MEDS

Woke in the morning not feeling right
Do I stay on earth, is it fight or flight?

Went to the cabinet, opened the door
Spilled my meds all over the floor

Was it blue in the morning and red at night?
Or was it reversed? *Fuck*, this wasn't right . . .

One was supposed to make me high, one was supposed to make me low
But if I mix them up, I wouldn't know which way I'd go

So because I've taken back my will
I always took that extra pill

Always trying to find the perfect mix
Maybe this time, *I'll do* the tricks

But it never seems to work the way I planned
My feet start to slip into the quicksand

So I take a yellow, an orange, and a black with blue
And I pray that this mix will get me through

The day that I finally decide to surrender
I go on again, that one last bender

And so the cycle will continue to spin
Or do I fight the devil within?

Out On A Cliff

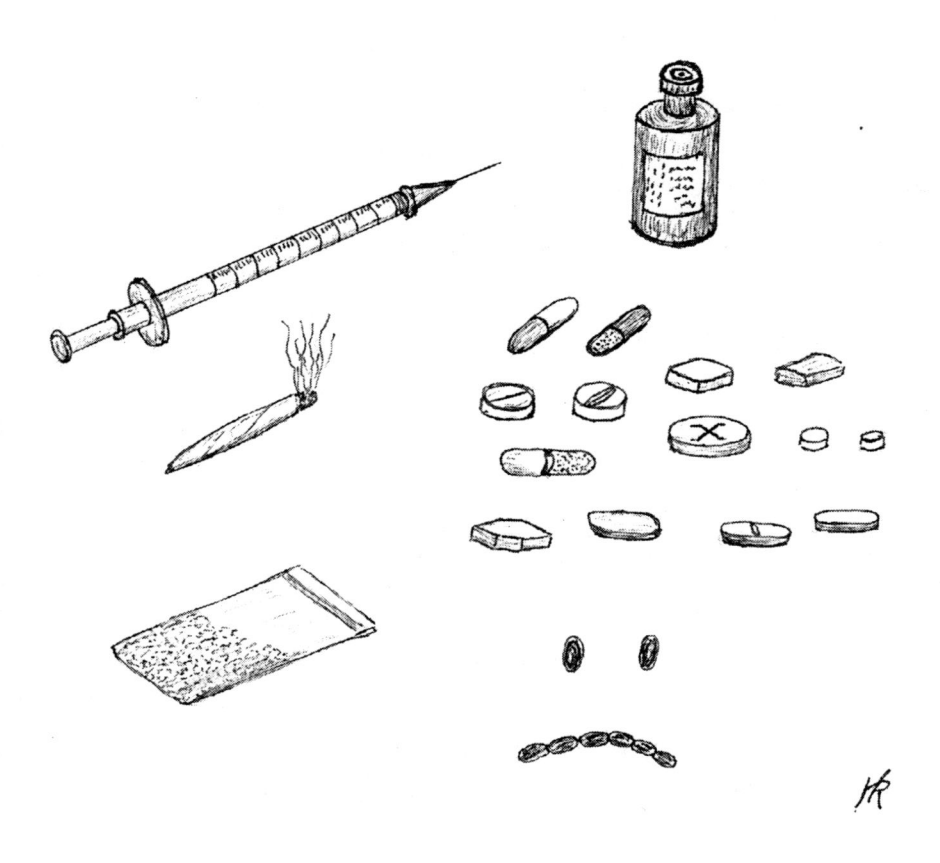

THE STAIRCASE

Went to the staircase, climbed the first step
That one's the hardest; be careful, don't trip

Took a couple more; they seemed to get wider
More questions, no answers; was I just an outsider?

And the wider they got, the more I wanted to know
But I didn't know how to ask; should I stay or should I go?

I ran up a little quicker, my sights fixed upon the sky
Got to get to the next level; if I don't, I might die

Don't look back down; it will only cause fear
I've lived that same nightmare, year after year

The higher I climbed, the better the view
No more misunderstandings; I knew what I had to do

Just a few more steps, I'm almost there
Remember what's around me, always be aware

Then I made the top step; it wasn't that hard
I finally stopped playing poker, got dealt the right card

Out On A Cliff

INSOMNIA

Lyin' awake, watchin' the clock count down
Gonna get outta bed, maybe walk around town

Unable to sleep night after night
Battling insomnia; what a terrible fight

Take a few tabs to shut the lights out
But I usually awake with screams and a shout

Night terrors arrive at the exact same time
Once I'm up and moving, I'm usually fine

My eyes rest, but my mind never sleeps
Damn those dreams; they give me the creeps

I'm trying to work through the cause of those dreams
Feels like I'm swimming up rivers and streams

One day at a time, I'll get through the pain
Got nothing to lose but everything to gain

Even though I hate to rely on the meds
Being on them forever is what my heart dreads

They're helping me walk through this spiraling hole
Can't get outta my head, feels like a downhill roll

I keep on trying to have thoughts of peace
Sooner or later, I'll get that release

When I'm finally able to keep calm in my heart
Then me and my insomnia will finally part

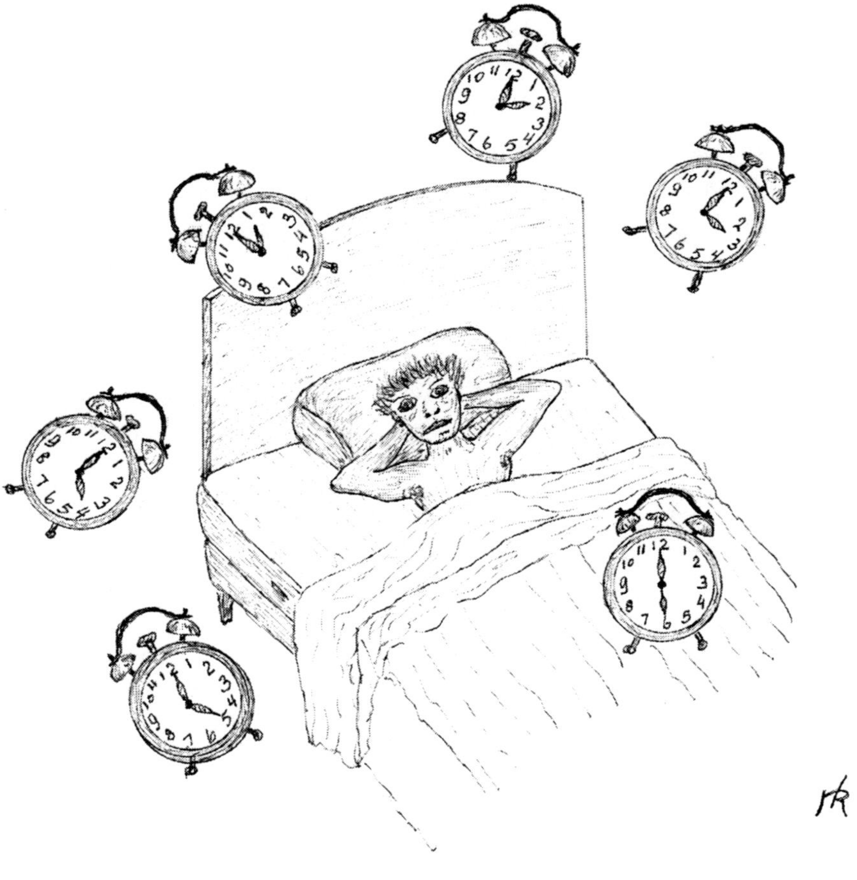

DRY DRUNK

I thought of a drink just the other day
It came on real quick, then it went away

With those kinds of thoughts, the alcoholic must deal
When it finally goes away, it's crummy how you feel

Some nights you dream and awake in a sweat
Not knowing, if I drank or why I feel like shit

They call it a dry drunk; each of us goes through it
It just seems so real; in your stomach, there's a pit

Your disease waits patiently on your shoulder, staying strong
Waiting for you to weaken, drop your guard, get the gong

So you hold on with all your might; your dignity is what he'll steal
You don't want it to beat you, but it just seems so real

The taste in your mouth, the hole in your gut, the fog in your head
It's too surreal; did I or didn't I get drunk? So you stay in bed

Eventually they're gone, those cobwebs in your brain
Then you pull yourself together, and you thank God you're sane

Out On A Cliff

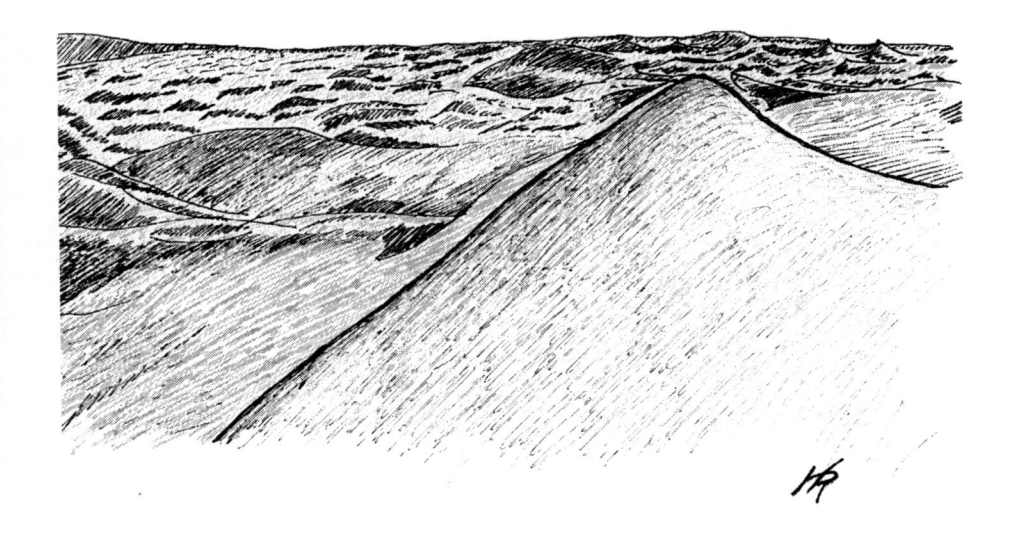

YESTERDAY

Yesterday is all but gone
Some memories good, some memories wrong

Things you wanted for yourself
Have all been placed upon a shelf

You fight the sadness of all failed dreams
You try to sew the ripped-up seams

Wearing your emotions upon your sleeve
Makes life's little miracles hard to believe

But the sleeves are torn, and the blood is flowing
The emotions you wore, you keep on showing

Showing them off for all to see
From high on a mountain or the top of a tree

And when someone says, "I know how you feel"
It becomes very clear that your pain is real

Then you start to drift back to that place in your head
Where all the sadness makes you feel dead

You fight every single inch of the way
But the pain is so real that you're starting to sway

Just as you're about to fall to the ground
You reach deep down, grabbing the strength you had found

A strength that is real as ten grown men
Then calmness arrives, and you locate your Zen

So you reach inside of your healthy toolbox
And suddenly remember you're smart as a fox

Then gratitude strikes for the lessons you learned
The lessons of yesterday, when your life got burned

Out On A Cliff

TRAPPED IN A TUNNEL

I was trapped in a tunnel, couldn't see the light
The walls were getting closer, knew I was in for a fight

Life's not always easy, journey's not always smooth
Sometimes you stumble through your day, sometimes you're in a groove

No matter what the circumstance, throw your shoulders back
You march on forward through your day, awaiting the next attack

It's not the paranoia that dictates your next step
You've been through this a thousand times, won't be no one's schlep

Your healthy paranoia turns to a healthy fear
It's kept you safe from day to day and month to month to year

Just when you think the tunnel's walls are about to squish you tight
A crack appears up in the distance, and you glimpse a ray of light

Now you find yourself going full speed to make it to the end
But suddenly the tunnel starts to move, straight line becomes a bend

So you slow yourself to a normal speed but keep your goal in sight
You've made it through the darkened tunnel and broke out into the light

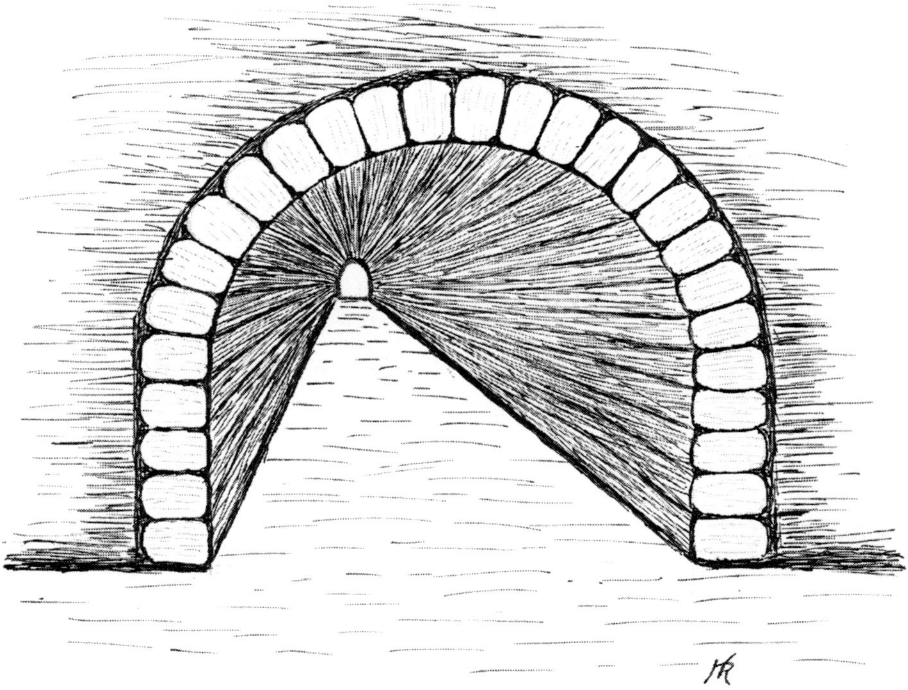

Gary Rubie and Henk Rubie

DEAR GOD

Dear God, it's been some time since we had a chat
We've talked about this; I've complained about that

I hope you're not mad I didn't call you sooner
But often I felt I was on the *Apollo 12* lunar

I was up in space, not with you but all alone
I didn't think you cared, thought you were hard as a stone

How could you let those things happen to me?
I was only a child, just barely past three

What was I to learn, what lesson were you teachin'?
I hated the church, the white collar, the preachin'

You caused me resentment for many long years
I hated your guts; I drowned you with beers

But even they took their toll, turned me into a drunk
Now what was I supposed to do? I became a filthy punk

So I came full circle and had to ask for grace
And there you were again. God, right in my face

So I'm broken and humbled; what are you gonna teach me now?
To step up to the altar, get down, and bow?

My sins are gone, my debts are paid
I asked for your forgiveness on my knees and prayed

But, God, I'm not the man I used to be
I know I have to ask for help, and for help I plea

Please don't let me down this time
The lessons you taught will hurt me a lifetime

I will try to talk to you every single day
Even though my feet still feel like clay

Out On A Cliff

Guide me through the toughness and give me a little light
Please let my life go smoothly so I don't always have to fight

Dear God . . .

EAGLE SPIRIT

My Eagle Spirit came and took me away
Flew to a place in my head where I wanted to stay

We soared together over rivers and lakes
Showed me my life, my victories, my mistakes

Showed me places I had yet to know
This made me anxious; did I really want to go?

My Eagle Spirit is my internal guide
When it is close, I listen, don't run and hide

My Eagle Spirit has saved my life
Flew me out of the canyon after being under the knife

When I woke up, I thought it was all a dream
But then I saw the nurse, and she said she heard my screams

I felt very confused for months, then years
Tried to sort it all out over whiskeys and beers

We talked a lot through those difficult times
He said I was sensitive to others' feelings and minds

He said it was special and I should practice much care
If my crown chakra was open, I would be left naked and bare

I let a dying woman get into my head
For a while after, I felt I was dead

I let the positive get sucked out and took the negative into my crown
There was a powerful force that entered me; it almost knocked me down

Shortly after I studied Reiki level 1 and level 2
That is when my ability to protect myself grew

Now when my Eagle Spirit arrives, I'm sensitive to his touch
There is a strong level of comfort when I'm in his clutch

Out On A Cliff

CLOUD

Lost in a cloud high above the earth
A hundred miles from the ground, searching for my worth

Look down at the city like insects in a nest
Hurrying to go nowhere, each one's like the rest

Sometimes in the clouds, it's easy to get lost
How bad do you want freedom, how much is the cost?

Get your feet firmly planted, put them both on the ground
But take nothing for granted, just go one more round

So when you're floating around and your cloud's looking pink
Remember the dangers of that very first drink

That first one will hit you like a heavyweight's glove
You'll be down on the canvas, not the clouds up above

As it starts to progress, through the canvas you'll melt
Then before it's too late, you won't know what's been dealt

Then the choices are tough; ride straight down to hell
Or go back to your cloud and decide to get well

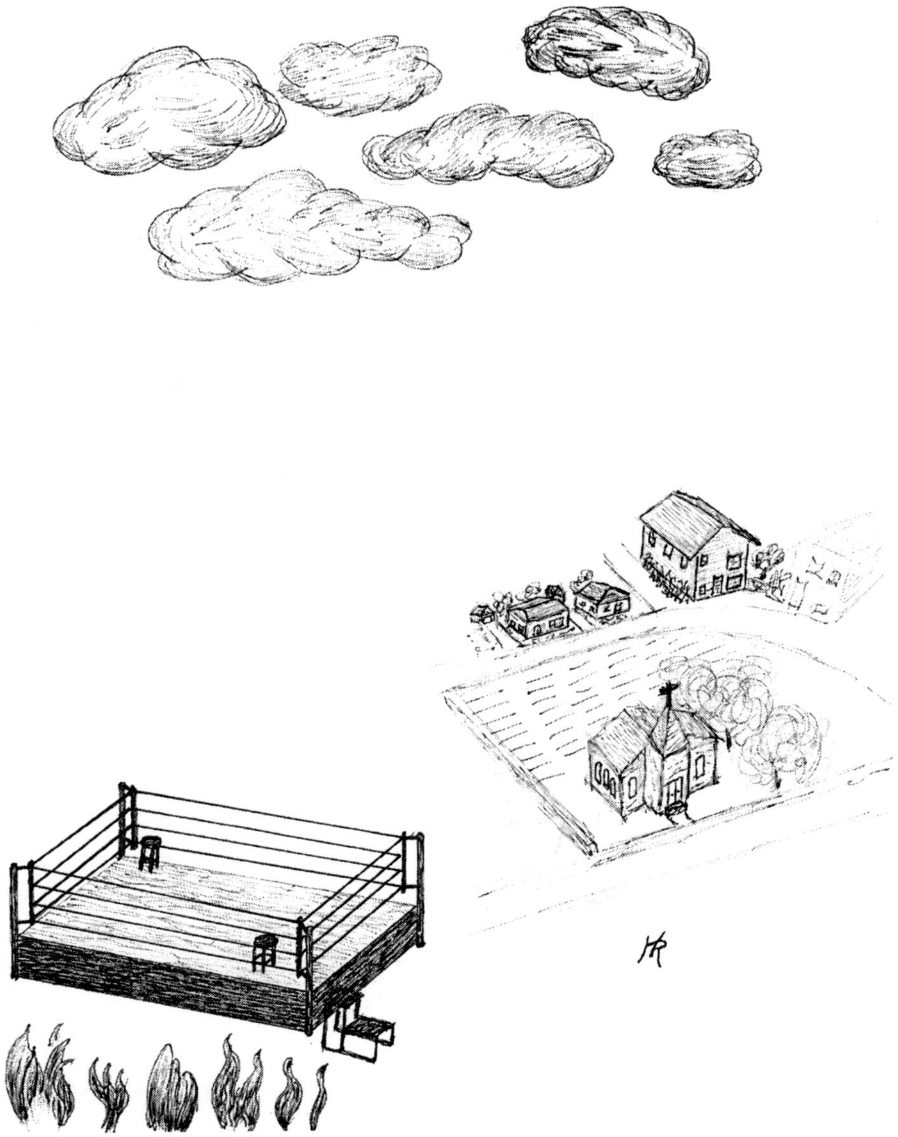

THE GAMBLE

Flip your coin up in the sky
Heads you live, tails you die

I lived to use and used to live
It mashed my brain, made my head a sieve

I fought the weather, the hail, the sleet
Victory lies in the admission of defeat

Had to go deep, find out where it began
Self-analysis is a difficult plan

Everything's structured to peel back the layers
You start and end each day with a new set of prayers

It seems the only path I'm supposed to take
Is if I walk with God; there'll be no mistake

And so the gambles we take each day of the week
Is to trust the system, don't play hide-and-seek

But if the system won't protect your right
They'll risk the chance of a major fight

An unstable patient left alone on the floor
They should boot their sorry ass right out the door

Why'd they gamble with our lives?
Like dodging the bullets and throwing knives

Till finally someone takes a stand
Then they're off the unit to another land

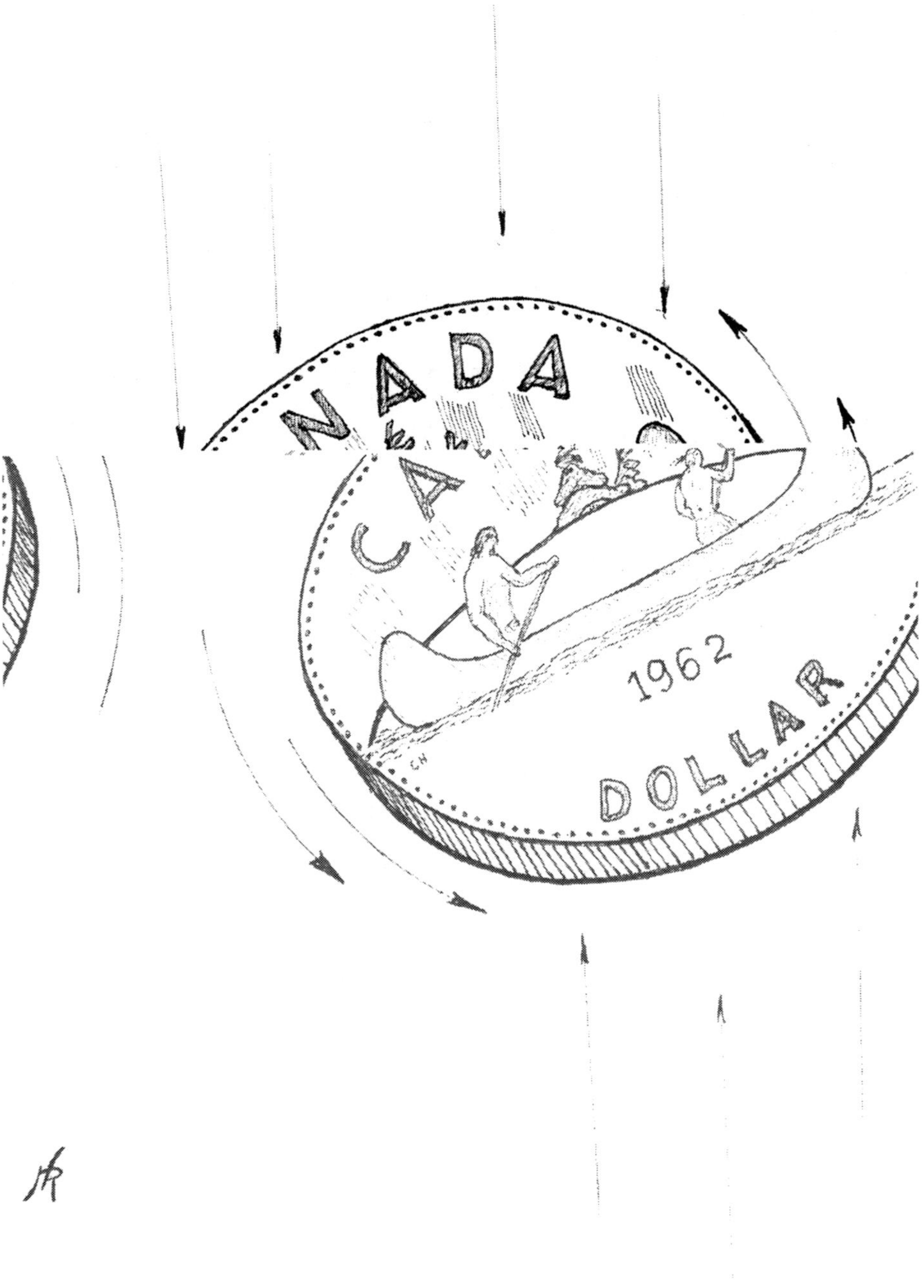
NADA
CA
1962
DOLLAR

THE YARD

You led me to the gated yard
I had no idea it would be this hard

The grass so green, flowers of light
My head couldn't conceive the colors this bright

I walked right in, like entering a maze
But all that I knew was this dark purple haze

My head started to flash, like lightning in the sky
Two weeks ago, I thought I would die

A quiet peace came over me
Told the gerbils in my head to let me be

They hopped right off, and things slowed down
"Not today," I said, "I won't be your clown"

So I took a deep breath and enjoyed the sight
Let go of the stress, enjoyed the light

The light is better than the darkness ever was
So now if I'm tempted, I'll say just because

The yard is green
I'm feeling clean

Out On A Cliff

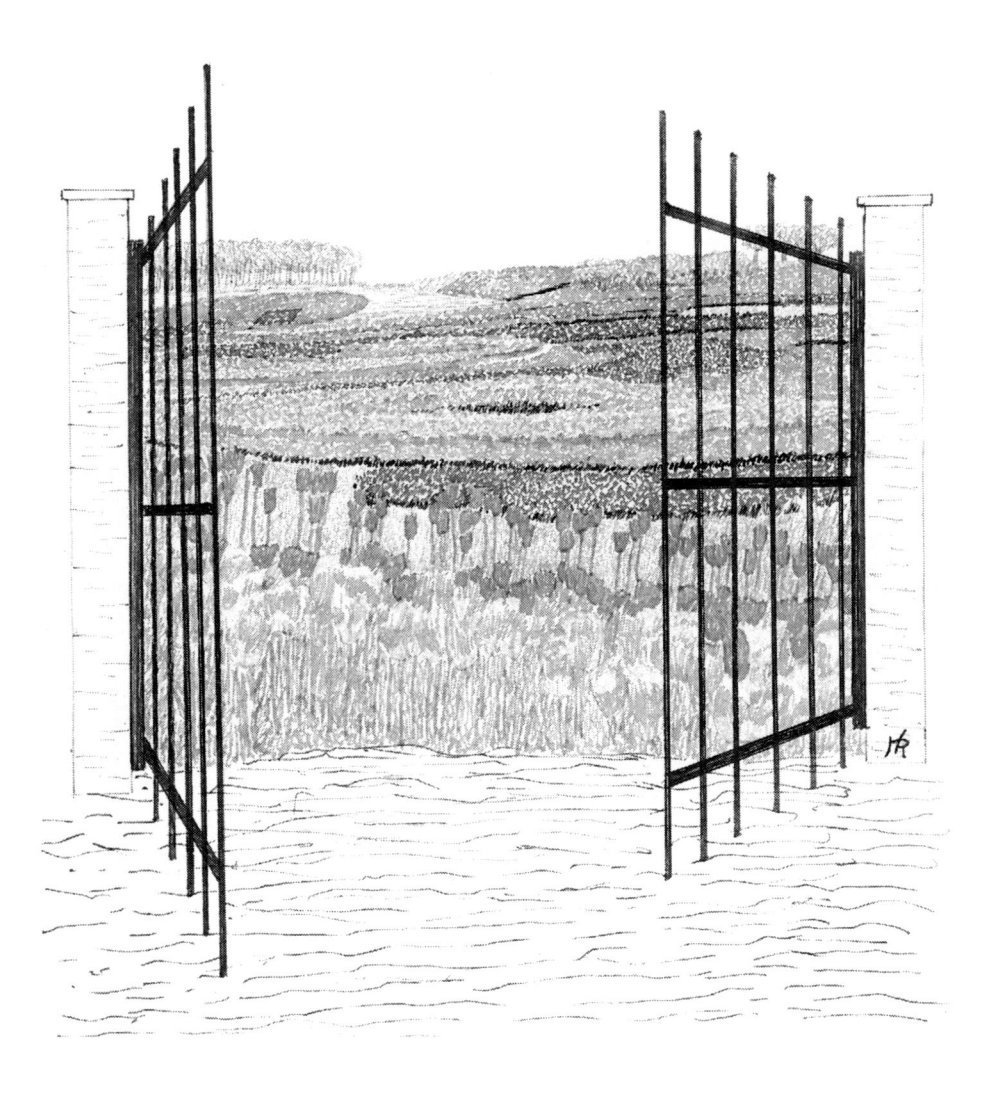

PENTHOUSE 11

Another long night in my hotel bed
Got nothing but time playing in my head

The mind stays busy, don't wander too far
Don't drift out to sea, don't slide to the bar

Time goes by slowly, all alone in a strange town
Don't let it get hold of you, don't wanna get down

Penthouse Eleven, this ain't all that cool
Nothing like heaven, now I'm the damn fool

I gotta start writing, clear my mind of those thoughts
Found a pen and a paper, looked inside at the dark spots

And then I started to write; I couldn't stop the pen
So I kept going to the dark place again and again

And when my mind slowed and I put down the pen
I had all of these stories; I wanted to do it again

So now when I go to Penthouse Eleven
I bring along this new book, and I trip off to heaven

PH11

GROUNDED

I can feel the roots growing outta my feet
I'm feeling real grounded; love the sun, love the heat

My feet are firmly planted in this soft ocean sand
Finally starting to mellow; I'm feeling quite grand

One week is too short; two weeks is too long
Ten days would be perfect; man, I'm feeling real strong

The sound of the ocean is calming my head
No need to lie low or hide in my bed

I'm in tune with Mother Nature; she's speaking real clear
It's a good way to live, without a belly full of beer

This is just what I needed; no pill could match
Seven days on the ocean, and I never felt a scratch

My Eagle Spirit is soaring, taking me high into the sky
For two weeks I haven't felt like I needed to cry

And although my heart's still racing and pulse is a little bit high
The anxiety has left me, and I don't feel like I might die

I can feel the roots growing; I'm grounded in the sand

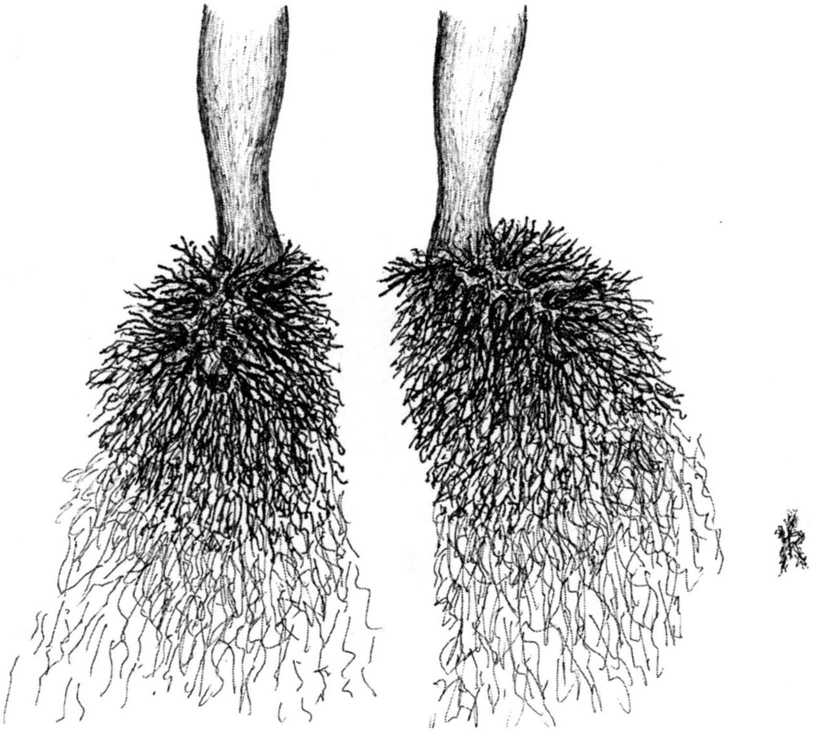

PORT OF MIAMI

Pulled into port, not sure what to expect
It was much like an airport, with customs and bag checks

A little confusing, turn left or turn right
Here's your bag and your badge, sir, go up one flight

We took our own bags as we walked 'cross the plank
Was a great idea since we didn't have to wait to say thanks

Unpacked right away, then had a life jacket drill
Showed us all how to survive if the boat took a spill

Once the drills were over, we went to the back of the boat
Watched the ship set sail, leaving Miami afloat

It was real calm and serene on the adult-only chairs
We watched the shoreline disappear with million-mile stares

Big water is hypnotizing from a gigantic ship
Makes you calm and serene and not seasick

The smell was incredible, fresh and clean with salt
Every breath you took made the anxiety halt

This just might be the smartest trip I've done
From the moment it started, we both had fun

Time goes by quick when it's with whom you love
So I breathe her in like the stars above

It's hard to explain the calm that I feel
But I'm not gonna question it; just enjoy what's real

Serenity was found . . .

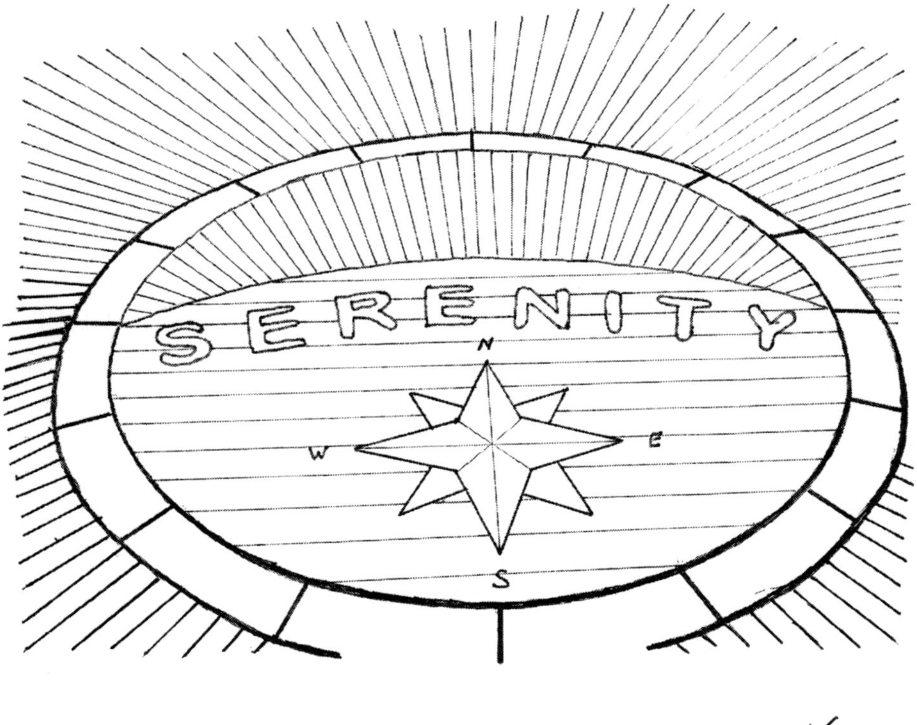
SERENITY
N
W
E
S

MY PAST

I have discovered that my past is the key, not the collapse
There were many struggles and a number of relapse

With every step ahead, there seemed to be two back
I couldn't escape the darkness; all I saw was black

But something happened; there was a significant change
I couldn't put my finger on it, just made me feel strange

It was a positive shift; my low energy got high
I can't explain the movement; I can't tell you why

When I'm working my program and things seem right
The steps come easy, and my whole world seems bright

My darkest secrets become my greatest gifts
Sharing with another gives him a tremendous lift

Telling a stranger of my twisted past
Makes his own strange life not seem so vast

It's how we relate in the world of recovery
When a newcomer gets it, he's got quite a discovery

It's funny how I used to beat myself up
I had to learn to love me like a baby pup

The newcomer walks a similar path
Until he loves himself and is free of his wrath

WHAT'S MY FUTURE?

What does the future have in store for me?
Have I paid my debt to society?

Must I put my ass in the electric chair
So they can fry my brain and burn my hair?

Do I have to give a pound of flesh?
Rob me of dignity, trapped in a mess

Life was unkind, so I always fought back
As though I were from the other side of the track

Voices screamed deep in my soul
Crawled a million miles over burning coal

I've been broken, beaten, and humbled to the bone
The war is over, and I'm all alone

I'm tired and scared, need to rest
Made restitution, did my best

Heads held high just above the cloud
Dignity returned; I'm strong and proud

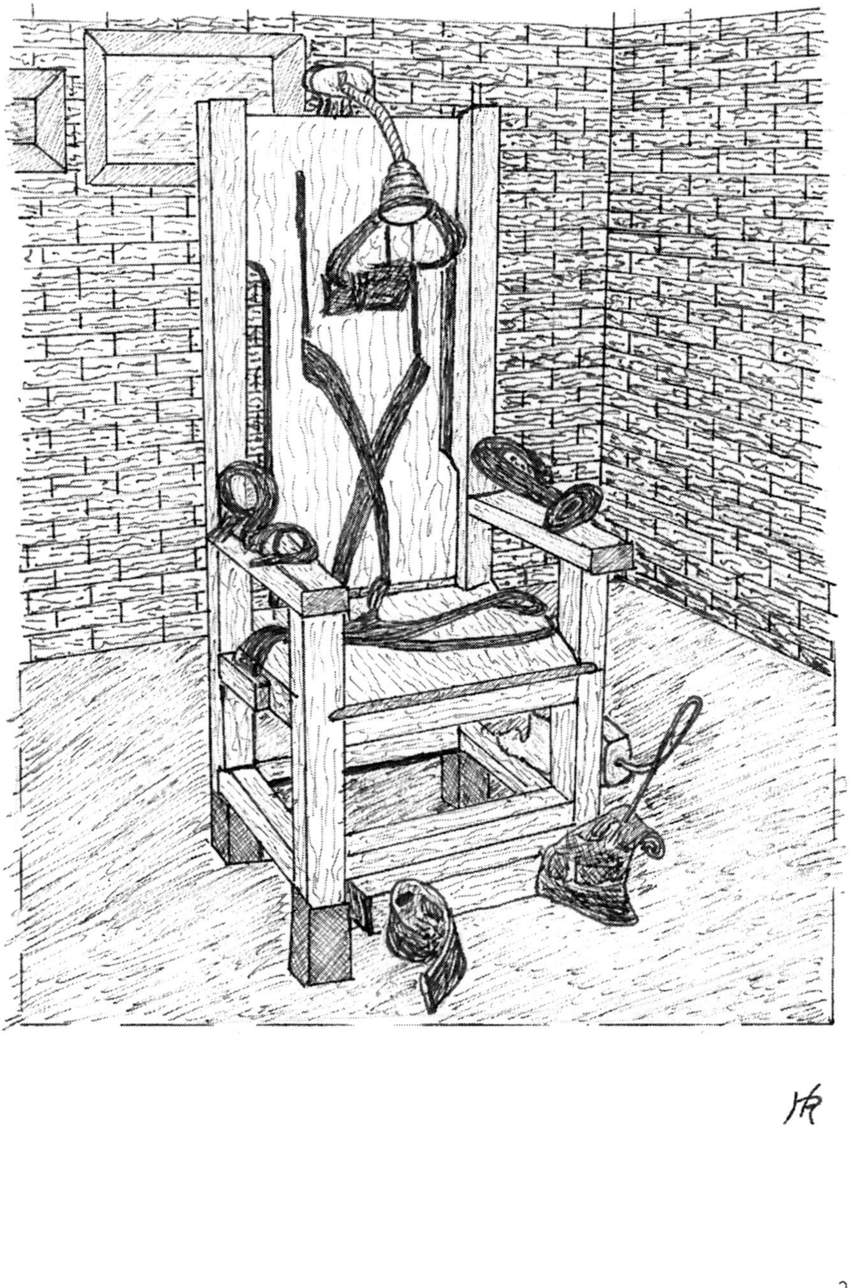

THE W.S.I.B. INTERVIEW

Can't slow down, brain's going too quick
Walkin' down the hall, made myself sick

So ramped up, nerves are shot
Been feeling this way an awful lot

Tried deep breathing and calming meditations
But they didn't work, so I took medications

The little yellow pill that slows it all down
Don't care if I'm judged, don't care if you frown

It's where I need to be at exactly this time
'Cuz when the interview's over, I'll be just fine

So the man shows up, and he's thirty minutes late
I'm beyond feeling anxious, got caught up at the gate

The interview starts and turns to interrogation
Am I in treatment or at the police station?

For over two hours, we talk about my pain
He thinks it's therapeutic; well, he ain't in my brain

I was cranked even more when the questions were done
Wasn't a walk in the park; this part wasn't fun

Had to give up names of friends who would talk
He went all the way; this guy wouldn't balk

So why don't I feel better, have some kind of relief?
Got exposed, stripped naked, opened up my beliefs

Out On A Cliff

So I've done my part, have to hurry up and wait
Nothing got resolved; the man went back to the gate

He'll pass the paper on; the decision's not his to make
Do they all have a grip on what's really at stake?

The interview's over; sit back, bide your time . . .

HOW TO RECOVER

I ask for help each morning and say thank you to God each night
There's a war that rages on within; some days, it's a terrible fight

I've learned to break my life down and live one day at a time
The days that that's too hard to do, then hours will be just fine

And when your struggles are so deep and painful, you don't think you'll last the hour
Just fill your glass with hope from God, and don't give addiction the power

You know the devil is on your shoulder, doing push-ups until you're weak
Fight back with all the strength you have; don't give him a chance to speak

Pick up the telephone and hold on to it real tight
You know it weighs a thousand pounds, but that call will help your fight

That's how the program works; it's what they taught us to do
Go to meetings, don't take the first drink, call your sponsor; he'll help you

It's a simple, uncomplicated program made for complex people
Take it slow, take it easy, read the Big Book on top of a church steeple

Out On A Cliff

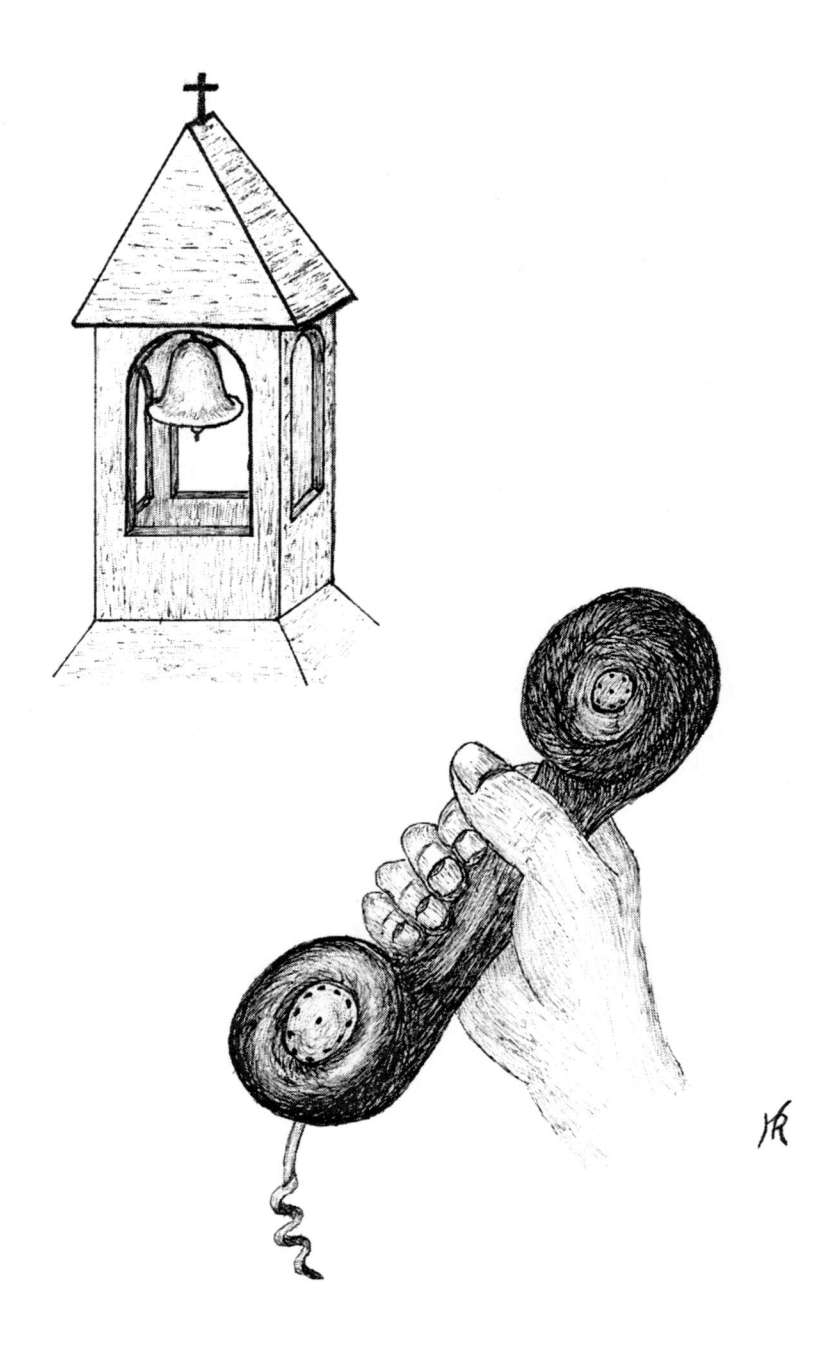

A CANVAS

Life is a canvas; you pick the paint
Put on gray and black or a soft red that's faint

The canvas is yours; no one else holds the brush
Have to slow your life down; don't always rush

Each day is a canvas, the picture of your life
Sometimes you go solo, other times with a wife

But be careful of your choices; the results affect many
They'll lend you a dime; for your thoughts, a penny

When you share what's in your head and let your guard down
The relationship becomes tight, or you end up becoming the clown

Being the artist isn't always the best role
Sure, you pick the paint, but there's always a hole

The hole is real deep, and you know that it's there
Always walking the same street, like you just don't care

So try to stay neutral, give someone else the brush
Let them pick the paint; with any luck, you won't blush

Out On A Cliff

Gary Rubie and Henk Rubie

A CLEAR HEAD

Didn't hear the sound
Two feet on the ground

I was feeling hope
Head without dope

Was there a storm outside?
Should I run and hide?

When the mind is clean
It works like a machine

Everything is clear
When you don't have beer

Then the lightning crashed
Was grateful I wasn't smashed

Now the storm was brewing
So much water, going canoeing

The best thing of all
When you don't stumble and fall

You can keep your family together
And, as one, you fight the weather

The kids will feel safe, the wife content
You'll hold them in your arms, strong like cement

There's a joy you will feel
'Cuz your life's become real

Nothing will match the gift you received
'Cuz you faced the devil and in God you believed

And you finally know you had good timing
'Cuz the clouds appeared with a silver lining

Out On A Cliff

MAYBE NEXT TIME I'LL GET IT RIGHT

The past is history; the future is a mystery
Now is a gift; that's why we call it the present[4]

Many a man has crumbled, living his life in the past and the future
They play in his mind like a game of roulette, pure torture

Stayin' where your hands are is the key to a good day
Remember, today is the tomorrow you worried about yesterday

Sometimes I slip, sometimes I fall, and sometimes each day is a terrible fight
Got to get off the "High Horse"; maybe next time I'll get it right

If I don't change, the person I was will drink again.
So slowly the transformation happens as I become a new man

Some days you grip and hold on so tight
You sweat through each minute, knuckles turn white

Other days are a breeze from breakfast to bed
The demon's asleep, which lurks in your head

It's where you want them to stay, in the dark in the back
If they suddenly awake, they bring on the panic attack

The child grew up, and the dreams went away
They were taken long ago, knew they wouldn't stay

I used to have a full building of crazies living in my head
Now they rent by the hour, trying to kill them off dead

Some days I live with such a terrible fright
If I try real hard, maybe next time I'll get it right

---

[4] Author to this phrase is unknown.

Out On A Cliff

Gary Rubie and Henk Rubie

ROUND THREE TREATMENT

I'm here 'cause I'm not all there
Wanted to run away, but didn't know to where

I have to stay; there is so much on the line
It's not about compensation; it's about my head being fine

I float in and out; my head does its own thing
Some days I'm grounded, some days on an eagle's wing

I'm trying so hard to string good days together
But some fill with sun, others have stormy weather

The pain that I carry I was taught is very real
For so many years, I had no idea how to heal

Then they tell me that PTSD won't kill me, but my addictions will
They share the same voice; you never know if it's laughter or a shrieking shrill

I'm open in group, but words come out like blame
The team challenges my recovery; I feel a great deal of shame

What am I to do? Now the meds got changed
I asked for the changes, but the changes feel strange

I want to be healthy; I'll do what it takes
The small voice deep inside keeps reminding what's at stake

Protect myself and be safe no matter the cost
Ninety days was suggested, but when it's done, will I be lost?

Patiently waiting for the neurologist to come in
Telling me my brain has a brown spot is where this doctor is to begin

A deeper study of the brain damage I sustained
From that fateful drunk accident when my whole life changed

Maybe she can help replace the missing spots
Help fix a shattered mind that can't remember a lot

Out On A Cliff

I came up with a plan I believe will keep me safe
It doesn't include being locked up for ninety days in either place

It's about taking back my life in a safe, gentle way
Being kind, caring, loving day after day

ROUND 3

GOOD-BYE, ADDICTION

Good-bye, my lover; good-bye, my friend
Thought we'd be together till the bitter end

We were together over thirty years
You were in my head, between my ears

You took me to places never thought I'd go
Had a crippling fear from my head to my toe

You helped me deal with all my failure
When I lost my house, had to live in a trailer

Anything I gained, good fortunes I earned
You stole those too; another lesson learned

You caused me poor health and made me quite ill
I followed your advice, always took the extra pill

You robbed me of love, took my wife and my kids
But I kept on following; you dumped me on the skids

No matter where I went, you were always there
You stripped me of dignity; you gave me white hair

You taught me to isolate and continuously blame
Minimized my role and crippled me with shame

I bargained with God, promised to give you up
But with each new bottom, you hid in my cup

So I say it again, and this time for good
Get out of my head; it's my neighborhood

Good-bye, my lover; good-bye, my friend
We won't be together 'cuz now is the end

Out On A Cliff

THE TRANSFORMATION

I saw a *butterfly* pass my way; the *transformation* was done
It hasn't been the easiest road; so grateful that I won

The *butterfly* begins the journey inside a *dark cocoon*
Waiting for the spring to come to see the *sun* and the *moon*

When it finally breaks out of its *shell*, it looks completely new
Not much different from where I came and the darkness I walked through

So now the *sun* shines on my face; I'm feeling warm and whole
When I look back from where I came, I saw life took its toll

The price I paid has made me strong and given me a *shell*
The *shell* protects me from day to night and keeps me out of *hell*

I float through each and every day, grateful for the smallest thing
Like watching the *butterflies* floating by and hearing the *songbirds sing*

My journey is completed now, no need to feel the hurt
Of a time in my life that I struggled and buried my head in the *dirt*

Today I'm a *beautiful butterfly* sailing over *Mother Earth*
The pain and the shame are behind me now, and I've regained my self-worth

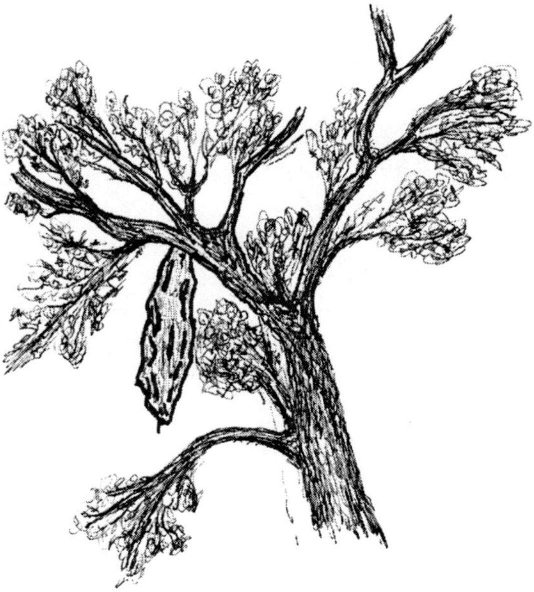

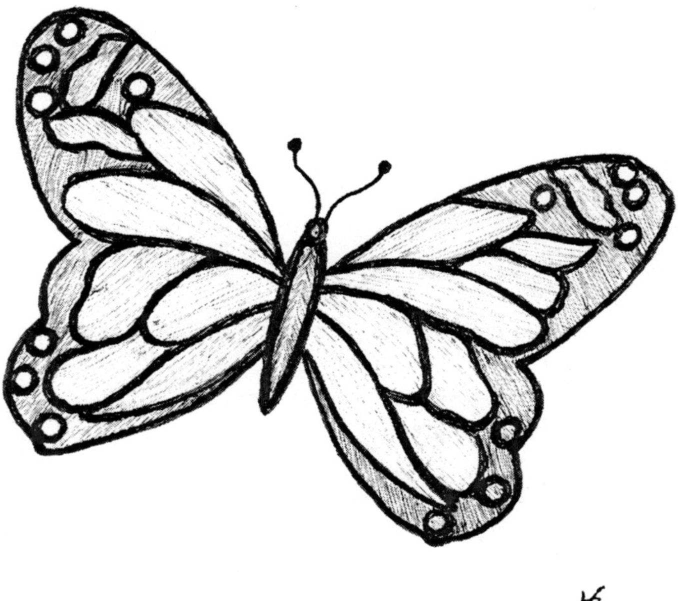

THE MASTERPIECE

When I first set eyes on the five stone pots
My mind drifted off to a faraway spot

Who made this masterpiece, from where did it come?
A handmade, one of a kind from a deep southern sun

Who is the creator—a man, woman, or child?
Is it from Mexico, South America, Peru, or the jungle wild?

A mystical piece forty to fifty years old
When I first set eyes on her, I had visions of gold

Many people asked, but no one received
When I shared my vision with Mitch, in me he believed

I was humbled and grateful when he said, "Go ahead, my son"
I knew exactly what I wanted, this would be fun

It took three weeks, but it was worth the wait
My selections were careful in order to seal the mystical fate

There's John Wayne, tiger jaws, golden barrel, and jade
The center's graced with a bromeliad; it's the crowning cascade

My masterpiece and I will never part
It's the constant reminder to slow down my heart

I was lost in a panic when PTSD ended my career
But when I quieted down, I knew my next stop was right here

So I owe a debt of a gratitude to Mitch and his staff
They helped stop my tears and taught me how again to laugh

This piece is dedicated to Mitchell Hewison and his staff Julie and Tami for their loving kindness

Out On A Cliff

Gary Rubie and Henk Rubie

CIRCA 1940

They came from east, travelled long from the west
Each one wore their Sunday best

They gathered together for family day
To see their loved ones, to eat and play

The day was sunny, not a cloud in the sky
It was hard to believe some gathered might die

Addiction takes no hostages, even back then
The late 1800s was when this house began

For that fleeting moment, when a camera took this shot
There was love and belief that not one would be lost

It doesn't matter who lives, doesn't matter who dies
Each one got a taste of those amazing blue skies

They paved the road for the thousands who followed
Their journey was tough; some lives got swallowed

The picture has color, and the symbolism is true
For every soul that entered, they didn't leave feeling blue

They will all remember that pretty sunny day
When the skies were blue and their families came to play

July 2010

This poem was inspired by the painting Family Day
Artist: Peter E. Snyder

Out On A Cliff

Gary Rubie and Henk Rubie

THE VISIT

We arrive uncertain at the wonder we were about to enter
We come to see where Dad has been; he'll take us to the center

The sheer size and unending hallways snake from the front to the end
It intimidates some newcomers, set on fifty-three acres of fledgling land

We follow our dad down the endless halls
See where he eats, sleeps, learns, and shoots basketballs

Then we leave the old stone building with the endless halls
Together we explore the enormous backyard hidden behind the gray walls

There are stairs and a road to guide you to the grass
They play badminton, tennis, horseshoes made of brass

The trees don't stop; there's a labyrinth made of thyme
A fire pit, a hope tree, a gazebo surrounded by pine

There are trails that go on for miles and miles
A winding river with tiny isles

And then he takes us to his favorite spot
A place to rest called the serenity rock

It's perfectly round and has two thick layers
Water bubbles from the top like hidden sprayers

And we sit and we stare on the Muskoka Chairs
Not a word is spoken; no one dares

When we break the silence, we talk about the stone
How it makes Dad peaceful, makes him feel like he's home

Out On A Cliff

The whole place was amazing; they even hang flowers
I think it helped Dad forget about the Twin Towers

We don't really understand the different things in his head
We pray to Jesus each day he doesn't end up dead

Heal Daddy . . .

SURRENDER

Back here again inside these hollowed halls
Asking myself, have I got the balls?

The balls to surrender to the demon alcohol
God's made it so clear after my last two falls

Time to get honest, to thine own self be true
Death is the option, so I know what I have to do

Take that eighteen-inch trip from my head to my heart
Have to share all my feelings; that's where I'll start

The time flies by quick, so I can't sit back
Gotta jump right in, don't fake it, don't slack

Ask God for help and go to every meeting I can
Do assignments, be on time, find structure and discipline

Reach out to the staff when I'm feeling pain
Complete surrender; no pain, no gain

The obsession has been lifted, can't explain the feeling
My ego has been crushed, and it has sent me reeling

Replaced by a humility so strong it's grabbed my heart
It's like my entire life stopped, then got a new kick start

A sense of peace and calmness that I just can't explain
Arrest and jail were part, then I saw the lecture on the brain

It seemed to all come together with an inner calm
Like the dark side of my brain blew up like a bomb

I like the change; it's making me feel fine
I know I've got to simplify, one day at a time

Out On A Cliff

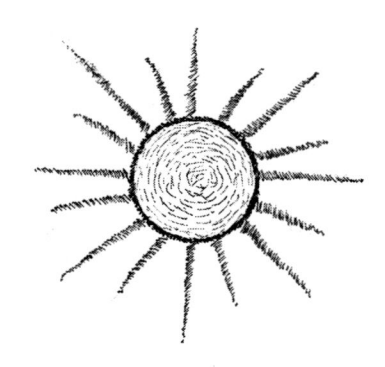

BREAKING THROUGH THE OTHER SIDE

I woke up early to beat the sun
Couldn't stay in bed, ain't missing any fun

Waking up clean, with no cobwebs in sight
Made me feel amazing, made me feel all right

I finally broke through to the other side
No need to run, no need to hide

Where was I last night? Where had I been?
I didn't have those fears; I woke up clean

The wall I had built with mortar and brick
Kept me hidden inside, kept me broken and sick

But I knocked the wall down, every last stone
Then realized something amazing; I wasn't alone

They were just like me; they broke through their own wall
Some did stumble, but a few didn't fall

And the strength in numbers picked the rest off the floor
We helped knock down their walls and walked them through the door

A bond grew tight, no man could break
For we all knew the cost, knew what was at stake

I left it all on the table, nothing else to give
I regained self-respect and my will to live

So I leave here today with an empty sack
Praying I stay clean and never have to come back

Out On A Cliff

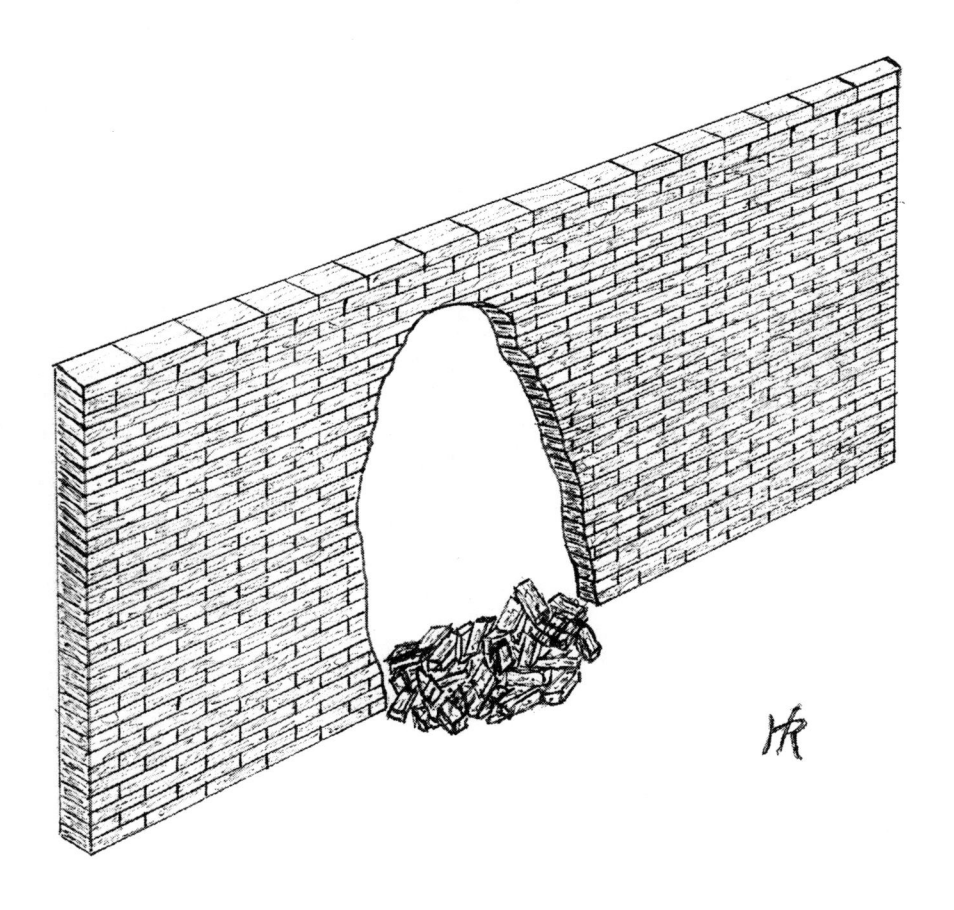

Gary Rubie and Henk Rubie

THE ILLUSTRATOR

Asked Dad for help; he said yes right away
Wanted sketches for my poems; he did a couple each day

When he started to draw, the illustrations were so real
It put a lump in my throat; he grabbed on to what I feel

I told him a lot would be simple and plain
He dove right in, didn't judge or cause me shame

He read them all before he started to draw
Some he read twice; he wasn't sure what he saw

I also shared that some likely would be dark
And the sketches wouldn't be a walk in the park

Even the ones that were disturbing, he didn't even flinch
He finished the illustration as though they were a cinch

It's been exciting to share this project with my dad
He seems to enjoy it like some fun he's never had

Now this trip is over, and we've grown real tight
Did this journey together; never once felt spite

No one could ask for a better dad on this land
'Cuz my dad's the best; he's absolutely grand

Out On A Cliff

Gary Rubie and Henk Rubie

YOUR CIRCLE

Proud does not express
The feelings I have for you
You have lived life to its fullest depths
You have concluded Dante's *Inferno*
Yet you have surfaced

You have surfaced with wisdom
A knowledge that creates your years
In which you have taken on every figure
From Zeus to a worm

You have sunk down a hole
And I envy that you came up without shame
You have reached darkness
One that few can understand

But those of us who are beginning
The cycle that is life
Look up to you
And aspire to become you

A person who has accomplished much
Yet who can relate to any tale
Who has stooped to many levels
Yet has always come out again

Uncle Gary, you are my muse
My inspiration to strive for excellence
An excellence that you may not see
But that you have accomplished
So now on your fortieth birthday
I thought it right to tell that I love you
And that what you have accomplished in the last forty years
Is what I hope to reach
An understanding and richness
That most people look for all their life!

Author: Ashley Barber-Gould (2002)

CONCLUSION

Well, if you made it this far, then I am totally impressed, because the trip nearly killed me.

Act One of my life has ended. A life lived in abundance, full of thrill and adventure, growth and self-destruction. A wonderfully tragic story. *That* life is over, however, and must remain there, in the past. Not to be ignored or forgotten. Although my experiences have scarred me, I will not allow them to cripple me.

The knowledge and wisdom gained in act one must now be applied to the new life I embark on, act two. Remember, you never really get over your tragedies and adversities; you simply move on and travel with those scars. Never squeeze them tightly; hold them gently. Self-discoveries have become abundant, and I am starting to recognize the map of my life; it's becoming visible to me, clearer to see a journey inward, one of self-discovery, one of peace and forgiveness (of self and others).

This journey shall define the legacy I will leave of my existence on this planet. I must never disregard the first forty-eight years, the foundation the building blocks I set to my new future. One that will be shared with many in richness of spirit and energy once the process of self-discovery has been fulfilled.

Whether you liked the book or not isn't relevant to me. That you read it and were open-minded enough to try and get a glimpse of the dangers of PTSD, depression, and addiction is most important. Policing was what I did for a living; it doesn't define who I am today.

If you have ever suffered from anything similar to what I described happening in my life, then I pray you have hope. Hope that you to will come out of the other side with self-respect and dignity. Those who struggle can identify with those who have survived.

I made it . . . You will make it . . . You just have to want to . . .

I will close this book by saying that I am still suffering full-blown post-traumatic stress disorder; however, with the help of my caregivers and, in particular, my friend Dr. Harry Vedelago, MSc., MD, CCFP, FCFP, ASAM, ABAM, I live a very normal and whole life today.

I remain on full disability and will retire from policing.

I have been given gifts in abundance in recovery. All obsessions and compulsions have been removed. I am living joyous and free of alcohol and drugs, clean, sober, and shameless in recovery.

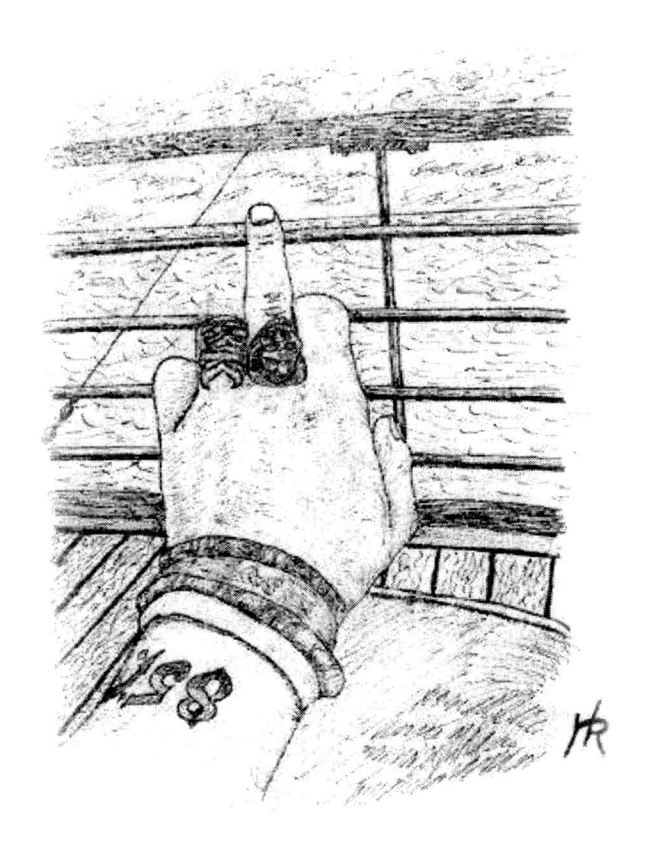

GOODBYE

.... and when it's all over & things come to an end
I owe a big thank you to those who stayed my friend ....

.... and to those that left me dry, or turned and walked,
A simple fuck you, and may we never again talk ...

INDEX

A

The alarm went off at 4:35; had Sunday day shift ahead, 154
Another call for service, middle of the day, 98
Another long night in my hotel bed, 246
As I fell out of the clouds, 202
Asked Dad for help; he said yes right away, 282
August 27, 1984, 82

B

Back here again inside these hollowed halls, 278
Back in the day, I worked in uniform patrol, 136
Balance and structure have not yet been found, 212
The base of the pyramid supports the peak, 110
Between the lines, I could not sleep, 162
The boat left the dock, 50
Broken hearts and broken dreams, 106
Brownie and Blackie couldn't be pulled apart, 138

C

Can't slow down, brain's going too quick, 256
The circus came to town just the other day, 158
The crack in the ground flung open wide, 172

D

Dear God, it's been some time since we had a chat, 236
Did I just see what I think I saw? Was what I saw real? 116
Didn't hear the sound, 262
Drove into Brampton to get me a gun, 188
Drove my truck to the edge of the cliff; the bottom did not look back, 184

E

The eyes tell the story of happiness or strife, 220

F

The fear starts to mount as the day draws near, 130
Flip your coin up in the sky, 242
Friday day shift, the last one's the best, 94

G

Gas in my gut, press real hard, 164
The gates slammed shut; I'd done it now, this time it was for real, 190
Good-bye, my lover; good-bye, my friend, 268
Got an older sister; her name is Diana, 22
Got off the plane, could feel the heat, 214
Got off the plane, fell flat on my face, 148
Got to the EX, dropped off my bike, 56

H

Had dinner with the family, then burned a big fatty, 104
A half dozen vodkas after work, liter and half of white with dinner, 92
Hands are sweaty, feet are cold, 218
He followed you into the bathroom stall, 100
The holes get deeper as I stumble and fall, 146

I

I asked for help; you arrived at the door, 16
I ask for help each morning and say thank you to God each night, 258
I can feel the roots growing outta my feet, 248
I can't explain the action you took, 66
I couldn't undo what I had done, 78
I fell down the church stairs but didn't feel the pain, 8
I gave and I gave, and you took and you took, 112
I have discovered that my past is the key, not the collapse, 252
I know you're frustrated, angry, and sad, 64
I know your pain; it sears like a knife, 4

I looked in the mirror and saw myself staring back, 150
I'm here 'cause I'm not all there, 266
I'm in the grip of something so strong, 216
In my head, I sometimes live, 166
I once had a friend named Mary Jane, 160
I saw a butterfly pass my way; the transformation was done, 270
I served your region and the citizens within, 118
I sit here alone, up high on my porch, 60
It doesn't matter how hard I try, 62
I thought of a drink just the other day, 230
It's Christmas Day 2009; a year has come and gone, 222
It started on the dance floor, 34
It started out just as a dream, 38
I walked through the door, shoulders slumped down, 198
I was a boy detective working in a suit, 90
I was so excited when the water broke, 44
I was the first cop on Peel to go online, 114
I was trapped in a tunnel, couldn't see the light, 234
I was walking out; you were walking in, 186
I woke up early to beat the sun, 280
I worked for two female rats at two different times, 120

J

The journey has taken you to many dark places, 124

L

Life is a canvas; you pick the paint, 260
Locked in a closet, couldn't get out, 140
Lost in a cloud high above the earth, 240
Lyin' awake, watchin' the clock count down, 228

M

Ma, you are wicked strong; you held us together, 20
A man lives his life that's long and full, 76
Many years ago, you did time with me, 30
Mirror, mirror on the wall, 180
A month has passed; we have become one, 70
My Eagle Spirit came and took me away, 238

N

No one's certain how the end really came, 86
No regrets for where I've been, 122

O

Oh, how I wish that the pain would stop, 128
One step forward, two steps back, 176-77
One thirty a.m.—911 call, 96

P

The past is history; the future is a mystery, 264
Picked up the phone and made the call, 192
Proud does not express, 284
Pulled into port, not sure what to expect, 250

R

The reaper paid a call just the other day, 156
Remember when we lay out on the grass, 10
Round and round and round we go, 134

S

Scars on my knees, scars on my face, 14
She was born on May 30, 1998, 48
Shopping for turkey was on Christmas Eve, 68
Sitting in a circle, sharin' what I think, 206
Sitting in a satin chair, 126
Sitting in the chair, waiting to be seen, 174
Sitting on a barstool, always bellied up, 142
Sittin' here in treatment, feeling lots of shame, 196
So a week's gone by, and we've done some time, 69
So much fury, so much pain, so much anger in my brain, 200
So there I sat in my black leather chair, 182
So you stumbled to the curb one last time, 168
Step up to the plate, take a swing, 210
Suckered to the head, knocked to the ground, 12
Swallowed my tongue, started to shake, 2

T

They came from east, travelled long from the west, 274
They sent me away to study for hours, 84

W

Walked down the beach, seen the old spot, 42
Walked in alone; the game had begun, 102
Walked in together; she couldn't stay, 40
The walk in the park became a run through hell, 74
Waves on the beach crash upon the ground, 178
We arrive uncertain at the wonder we were about to enter, 276
Well, I had to go away to get myself well, 71
Went to the Eiffel Tower; all I could see was you, 32
Went to the staircase, climbed the first step, 226
We sit around the table's square, 204
We travelled the road together, through the darkness and the light, 72
What a gift I've been given, second chances received, 208
What does the future have in store for me? 254
What were you thinking when you took it away? 6
When I first set eyes on the five stone pots, 272
Where did you go, you old skitter-bug? 58
Woke in the morning not feeling right, 224

Y

Yesterday is all but gone, 232
You gave everyone you touched, 54
You got run down as the daylight set, 26
You led me to edge of the cliff; my fear of heights was gone, 152
You led me to the darkness, 144
You led me to the gated yard, 244
Your mother screamed, "My water's broke," 46
You sent me out to work in the dark, 88
You thought you walked the righteous line, 108
You've caused lots of pain and told many lies, 170

AUTHOR'S PROFILE

Gary Rubie was born in Kitchener, Ontario, Canada, in 1962. He joined the Peel Regional Police Department in 1984, where he served for twenty-five years on a variety of frontline and plainclothes units. He enjoyed many successes in his career, being recognized sixty-four times with letters of appreciation from the public, police commendations, and awards. He continued his studies, taking thirty-three job-related courses over his career. In 2009, in his twenty-fifth year of policing, he was diagnosed with job-related career-ending post-traumatic stress disorder and was placed on permanent disability.

Henk Rubie was born in the Netherlands in 1931, where he was educated and joined the air force for two years. He worked as a toolmaker until he married his wife of fifty-three years, Antonia Rubie. Together they immigrated to Kitchener, Ontario, Canada, in 1959, where they raised three children. Henk worked for years as a skilled machinist in the RMS Machinery Division at the Uniroyal tire manufacturing facility in Kitchener. He retired in 1991. A boatbuilder by hobby and artist, he further honed his artistic skills and began oil painting, creating intarsia woodcrafts and continued building scale-model sailboats.

Gary's journey to writing poetry began just over seven years ago as a method of writing journals. With no formal training, he found solace in rhyme. It was a therapeutic way of putting his feelings on paper about the struggles and challenges he faced during his policing career and in dealing with the severe job-related trauma (PTSD) and his addictions.

Gary asked his father two years ago if he would consider drawing images to go with each poem, and the result is this one-of-a-kind collaboration between father and son. The poems have all been complemented with pen-and-ink illustrations done by Henk.

Gary's father believed in him. He felt this was his small way of working with and helping his son to find some relief from the crippling symptoms of his PTSD. With poetry and illustration, this memoir describes Gary's life journey through intense introspection and self-discovery to reveal a very intimate and personal path to recovery and a light of hope for all who may struggle.

CPSIA information can be obtained at www.ICGtesting.com
Printed in the USA
LVOW112021080612

285308LV00002B/36/P